Echoes of a Life Well Lived

*A Collection of Personal Stories, Essays, Poems, Insights,
Reflections and Observations*

Richard M. O'Bryan

Echoes of a Life Well Lived
A Collection of Personal Stories, Essays, Poems, Insights,
Reflections and Observations

Copyright © 2013 by Richard M O'Bryan.

This is a work of fiction. All of the characters, names, incidents, organizations, and dialogue in this novel are either the products of the author's imagination or are used fictitiously.

Because of the dynamic nature of the internet, any web addresses or links contained in this book may have changed since publication and may no longer be valid. The views expressed in this work are solely those of the author and do not necessarily reflect the views of the publisher, and the publisher hereby disclaims any responsibility for them.

Printed in the United States of America.

By

Beggars Tomb Press

All rights reserved.

ISBN: 0615974929

ISBN-13: 978-0615974927

Library of Congress registration pending

FOREWORD

I was actually first given the privilege on reading *Echoes of a Life Well Lived: A Collection of Personal Stories, Essays, Poems, Insights, Reflections and Observations* one afternoon in July after I had picked Richard up at the airport in preparation for a book signing he was doing for his then current book *Josh & Me* and a speech he was going to give at Oak Hill Friends Meeting. Richard had gotten settled in the guest room at Beggars Tomb and handed me a three ring binder containing the rough draft in it. Richard knew that I had already read *Josh & Me* and seemed anxious to get my opinion on the collection he had handed me. I opened the binder and began reading and re-reading some things.

Upon finishing the last poem I had a satisfied feeling, like I had just eaten a good meal. The words, ideas and feelings flowed thickly like honey and nourished my soul with meaning and relevance as I was treated to a glimpse into Richard's soul. I really did not want to give the binder back! I wanted to keep it and read it again and again.

Writing is an extremely personal thing and it takes great courage and resolve to publish any work as you are essentially bearing your soul to the world and opening it to ridicule, but courage and honor are something that OB has in abundance. *Echoes of a life well Lived*, does live up to its title as it provides insights and observations that took a lifetime to accrue.

One of my favorite things in the world was to sit on the front porch and listen to old folks tell about their lives! In this book you get a rare opportunity to sit on the front porch with Richard as he relates the stories and wisdom that are the very fabric of his life.

When Richard asked me to write a foreword for *Echoes of a Life Well Lived*, I was honored but also a little nervous about trying to sum up such a touching and insightful work in a few mere sentences. I kept referring to it as the "poetry book" which aggravated OB a bit as he scolded me again and again, "it is not just poetry!" But in a sense it is all poetry as it captures the rhythm of his heartbeat.

John Kennedy once said, "When power leads man towards arrogance, poetry reminds him of his limitations. When power narrows the areas of man's concern, poetry reminds him of the richness and the diversity of his existence, when power corrupts, poetry cleanses." Richard has succeeded in giving us a reminder of the power and healing nature of poetry as his words touch the soul. I have had the great honor and privilege to get to know Richard as a fellow writer, a political commentator and above all and more importantly to me a friend and brother and here I can tell him that, "I love you back more!"

Mike Bodenheimer
beggarstomb.net

CONTENTS

POETRY

ABOUT THE AUTHOR

DEDICATION

Mr. John W. Selby My First Great Teacher and Mentor

Mike Bodenheimer - A Man who Defines by his life the Virtues of Pure Generosity, Scholarship and True Charity I am so HONORED to call him My Friend and My Brother.

Dylan L. Austin - One of the Most Gifted and Talented Young People I have ever met. He has Become My Little Brother through the LOVE and GRACE of God and I have the Privilege of being his Big Brother and Mentor through that same Love and Grace. He will make this world a Better Place because he Shares His Gifts, Talents and Himself freely and openly.

My Friends and Brothers through "YouNow": the Best Site on the Internet

Adi Sideman	*Richard Robert Aten Jr. USMC*
Josh Twelves	*Christian Augustus Braddley*
Matt Thomas	*Matt Cava*
Rob Gallo	*Nick Mason*
Joe Pasquale	*Dave Hodges*
Skyler Shephard	*Ben Frasier*
Erick Wolf	*Robert Matthews*
Todd Wooten	*Cole Tibbs*
Dylan Swain	

"HONOR MORE"

MY FATHER THE RAT AND THE WIRE

Something that I have never quite understood in my life, and I think this may be the case with most young men, is that we often feel we really don't have all that much in common with our fathers, at least while we are still living at home. This commonality only seems to come to light the older and wiser we get, unfortunately, sometimes, after it is too late.

This is the way it was with my father and me. Even though he had very little formal education, he was a genius when it came to mechanical things. He could tell you what was wrong with an engine simply by listening to it. He could go into almost any store, see a piece of furniture, and come home and reproduce it from memory. I do not know what happened in the evolutionary scheme of things, but not one of those genes was ever passed down to me.

I can remember the very first time my father asked me to get him an Allen wrench from his tool box. I thought he had named his tools, i.e., he had an "Alan" wrench and a "Phillip" screwdriver. It seemed logical, even if a little formal to me. My father's response to this lack of genetic engineering was constantly to thank God that his second son had been born with a brain, because his hands were useless.

So as you can imagine, while in the presence of my father I shied away from any task that had to do with tools, mechanics, building, or electronics. It wasn't that I was lazy; my motivation was purely for the safety of myself and others around me. As a result, there were very few times when I was growing up that my father and I ever shared a task of this nature. The few times that we did, however, had the makings for some of the funniest and most enjoyable experiences in my life.

The following is the story of one of those times. I call it, "My father the Rat and the Wire!"

I will assume that most of you were not raised on a farm or in a rural area. Therefore, I feel it necessary to give you a little background into some of the little-known nuances of agricultural life in order for you to truly understand and enjoy this story.

On the farm where I grew up, the main crops were corn, wheat, rye, and barley. Besides these grains being a great source of income, they are also a source of food for many creatures that dwell on the farm – creatures that, for the most part are harmless, and provide an unseen benefit to the farm.

There was one creature, though, that provided absolutely no benefit whatsoever and was always most unwelcome: the rat. The only reason this gray furry creature was even tolerated was because there were too many of them to eradicate. For three seasons of the year they were almost never seen. It was only in the cold winter months that they made their presence known within the confines of a farm house. As long as they kept hidden, their presence was tolerated. They entered the house for two main reasons: one, to get away from the cold temperatures, and two, to try to find a new food source, because by this time the grain was usually gone.

I can honestly say that I never saw a rat in our farmhouse. Their presence was usually betrayed by the sounds they made. They would enter the house from some unseen hole in the foundation and then proceed to pass the winter months in the walls and attic. They were opportunists when it came to food and could eat and survive on almost anything that they found. Rats give entirely new meaning to the word *omnivore*. Their noisiness is what usually brings them into conflict with human inhabitants, and this is where our story begins...

If I recall correctly, the trouble began in about mid-January, when I was about 12 years old. We had gone through an unusually long cold spell, and I believe this is what caused the multiplication of the population of rats in the house. The farmhouse where I grew up was very old, very large, very open, and very accommodating to these gray, long-tailed devils. Originally the house was heated by fireplaces and woodstoves and had no electricity. But as time passed, the house was dragged into the modern world, whether it liked it or not. An oil furnace was installed, and the house was also wired for electricity. All of the fireplaces and wood stoves were removed and the opening in the wall was bricked over or covered up. But what was unseen and unknown is that the main electric cables had been run in most of the chimneys. This would have been a very useful piece of information for my father, but had he known this there would be no story!

So in this bliss of electrical ignorance the seeds of a great disaster had been sewn many years before. The main chimney of our house had been in our living room, which happened to be directly under my parents' bedroom. Here is where the trouble began. My father, who was never known

3

for his acute sense of hearing, began to complain that he couldn't sleep at night because somewhere in the chimney of his bedroom he could hear what he claimed to be a gigantic rat chewing on something. I always marveled at his ability to describe this monster in such great detail, without ever actually having seeing the fabled creature. When I tried to explain to him with all of my education and vast experience that rodents in North America never got that large, his only response was to tell me to be quiet and mind my own business because he knew much more about this particular matter than I did.

Now here was an example of something that puzzled me about our relationship. I thought I was the one with the book learning and he was the one with the mechanical ability. But in this instance he was claiming both as his domain of expertise. And at the age of 12, who was I to argue? Especially with the man who was twice my size and almost three times my weight. So I just bided my time for my moment in the sun. You see, I believe that there is justice in the world between kids and adults and that, over the course of time, everything balances out. And that is exactly what happened.

As the days and nights began to drag on, my father complained of an ever-increasing state of fatigue brought on by the fact that he could not sleep because of the noise the rat was making in the chimney of his bedroom. He tried many things over the next few days to resolve the situation. These attempts ranged from simply banging on the wall of the chimney, to the extreme of going up on the roof and dropping left over smoke bombs from the Fourth of July down the open vent. Having survived neither cracked walls nor great fire from these attempts, I consider them harmless. What I really didn't count on was my father's determination. This battle between man and rat became a very personal one. I doubt that even the great Crusaders had more resolve and determination to find the Holy Grail than my father did to get rid of that rodent.

I began to see a change in my father's demeanor and attitude when he would begin to talk about this problem. A glaze would come over his eyes, his face would flush, and he would begin to bang on the nearest flat surface.

I need to point out something here again for enlightenment and for the understanding of the reader. As I stated earlier in the story, my father did not have a great deal of formal education; therefore, his vocabulary lacked the number of adjectives that are more readily available to the more book-read, shall we say? But those that he did have and the way he used them made up for what he lacked. In some situations, when properly motivated, my father could paint a more colorful and powerful picture than most well-known and recognized Renaissance painters. I guess what I am trying to say is that my father's language was often colorful but not the kind you'd want to use in mixed company.

With that said, seldom to that point in my life had I ever heard my father express so many colorful words towards one of God's lowly creatures. This kind of colorful language was usually reserved for when he was by himself and accidentally hit his finger with a hammer or dropped something heavy on his foot.

As the days went on, my dad was not able to stop the noise in his bedroom. He became almost manic for a solution. Then at the end of January he came in from work with a strange sort of calm about him that I hadn't seen for many days. He announced that he had finally figured out how to eliminate his dreaded enemy in the chimney. When I asked him to explain what he was going to do while we all ate dinner that night, he silenced me by saying it was very technical and that I wouldn't understand. I would just have to watch and see what happened and try very hard to learn something from it. Once he said this, I thought that I was free from participation in his great scheme. But I was mistaken.

We were in the television room at about 8:30 that night when I saw my father sit upright in his chair. He looked like one of our German short-haired pointer dogs who had just come upon the world's largest covey of quail. I had never seen my father in that posture before; it was as if he had become frozen or hypnotized. When I inquired as to what was wrong, he told me to be quiet and listen. When I asked him what I was listening for, one quick glance from those focused eyes told me any further words from my lips could be fatal.

I then watched as my father silently turned in his chair 90 degrees to face the living room. He then slowly rose and with the stealth of a great cat begin to creep to the wall making no sound whatsoever until he had reached a spot just inches in front of the chimney. I'm not exactly sure, but I thought I heard him say to himself, "Now I've finally got you!" Then it dawned on me: he wasn't talking to himself; he was talking to the unseen monster he sensed just on the other side of the plaster. His great plan was about to be put into action!

I watched my father back away slowly and silently, step by slow step, until he felt he was out of the hearing range of the rat. He turned and walked out of the room to retrieve something from the summer kitchen. He quickly returned with two new objects: one, a 22-caliber pistol, and two, a brand-new stethoscope. Once more he silently approached the wall. When his head was only a matter of inches from it, he turned slowly and signaled for me to join him. So with my ninja training, I carefully crept over and joined him in the living room, trying as hard as possible to look supportive and not laugh out loud.

Now, as I stated before, my strong point in this

relationship was book learning; therefore, I was expected to be more insightful, intuitive, and able to figure out complex cerebral plans very quickly. It didn't take me long to figure out what my father's plan was, because it required neither insight nor intuition. Basically what he was going to do was to use the stethoscope to precisely locate the rat on the other side of the plaster. Then, as God's appointed executioner, he was going to use his firearm to dispatch this hated creature back into the loving arms of its Creator. Did I say complex? This wasn't even connect the dots!

Now, being the educated one, I could instantly see many problems and ramifications with this plan. Then again, being only 12 years old and under an imposed vow of silence, I could only stand and watch the disaster unfold before my eyes.

I watched my father slowly raise the end of the stethoscope to the wall and, with all of the measured movements of the skilled surgeon, precisely locate the source of the noise caused by that hated creature. I saw my father's eyes light up when he had zeroed in on his unsuspecting, munching prey. He then slowly raised the pistol and aimed it at a spot directly beside the end of the stethoscope.

Because I was not concentrating as intently as my father, I knew instantly what was about to happen. At this point even if I had been allowed to speak I don't think I could have, because when you are 12 years old and see that your father is about to make a really dumb mistake that you will be able to hold over his head for the rest of his life, there is something deep inside that will keep you speechless.

When both the end of the stethoscope and the barrel of the pistol were in proper place, I saw the most evil and maniacal grin that I had ever seen cross my father's face. Then, with the precision of the best marksman, my father slowly and gently squeezed the trigger.

First came the loud explosion accompanied by a brilliant flash of light. At the same instant, my father screamed at the intense noise that had entered deep into his ears and brain from the end of the stethoscope, which he had forgotten in his haste to remove from near the end of the pistol. Just as suddenly the entire house went pitch black. Unknown to my father over the previous two weeks, his evil, gray, furry long-tailed monster enemy had been methodically chewing on the main power cable that years before had been run up through the hollow chimney rather than through the walls of the house.

My father turned out to be a much more perceptive man in this situation than I gave him credit for. Within a millisecond of the house going black and him losing his ability to hear high and low notes and pitches on the sound scale, I heard his voice somewhere in that great darkness directed at me saying, in a very emphatic and somewhat threatening manner, "Don't say a word. Don't even open your mouth, if you know what's good for you."

I don't understand why he thought I might provide commentary that could be in anyway interpreted as un-supportive. But what he could not possibly see or understand within that great darkness is that I did not have the ability or self-control to make any coherent sound because I was laughing convulsively and rolling uncontrollably on the floor.

I don't know how much time elapsed, but eventually my mother appeared in the room with a flashlight and asked what had happened. My father, with his impaired hearing, replied several times with ever-increasing volume what she had said before he finally understood my mother's question. Then he replied in a very loud voice that the rat had chewed through the power cable and caused the lights to go out when he killed it.

The only effect that this new version of the truth had on me was to make me laugh harder than I ever thought possible. Then, in a very loud voice, my father asked my mother for the light and left the room to retrieve some unknown objects, but not before kicking me as he stepped over me. In the years since, I have always thought his explanation of the kick as being accidental was suspicious, but I gave him the benefit of the doubt.

After an undetermined amount of time he returned with his toolbox, a large bucket with unknown contents, and a broom. In a loud voice, because he still couldn't hear, he told me he would need my help for little while. By this time I recovered enough to once again stand on my own two feet, and I walked over to him by the wall. Then he handed me the flashlight and told me to focus it on the spot on the wall where the bullet hole was. He kept complaining and told me to hold the light steady, but this is somewhat impossible when you are racked with waves of convulsive laughter. After a few of his sharp elbows to my ribs, however, I was able to gain some control of my motor skills and hold the light somewhat steady.

My father then proceeded to use a hammer and chisel and made a fairly large hole in the wall where the bullet had entered. This exposed the electric wire that was now in two separate pieces being held together only by one small strip of insulation. My father saw this as proof that he had not caused the blackout directly. He declared that what actually happened was that he had shot the rat and that the rat had pulled the wire in half in his last dying action out of spite.

So I inserted the flashlight and my head through the hole and, being able to see the entire chimney from its opening in the roof to the floor of the basement, I asked my father, then where is the rat?

He then told me that I was on very dangerous ground and to stop asking so many questions. But when you're 12 years old you have this sense of invulnerability about yourself, especially when you know you're going to be able to tell this story to everyone in your family many times over for the rest of your life, every time your father gets out of line. So, throwing caution to the wind I dared ask my father another question. If the rat had chewed that far through the wire, I asked, why didn't it electrocute him? My father shot me an icy stare and told me to be quiet because the question was too technical and I knew nothing about electricity. After another swift elbow to my ribs I got the message.

Well, it didn't take long for my father to restore the power to the rest of the house, because what little he knew about invisible rats behind plaster walls was more than adequately made up for through his ability to splice together power cords separated by random gunshots.

No matter how many times I've told this story, each and every time it carries me back to that instant with my dad. We laughed about that so many times in my life that I can't count them. My father has been gone for many years now, and as I think back over my life when I still had him with me, no matter how at odds we were the mention of that story would always restore peace and harmony.

I believe Mark Twain once said that when he was 16 he thought his dad was one of the stupidest people on earth. Yet when he was 21 he couldn't believe how intelligent his father had gotten in just five years. I can very much relate to this statement, because many times in my life due to our different interests and lack of common ground, I did not give my father all of the credit he truly deserved. In hindsight, I can see that this was one of my greatest errors. But being able to remember and retell the story, and to still remember and can convey the laughter and joy that it brings, is like a remedy to those faults.

When you are 12 years old you pretty much take things and situations pretty much at face value without looking too deeply into them. But with the passage of time and the acquisition of wisdom, you realize that every moment spent with your mother and father was deeper than it seemed.

And so it is with this story. I thought my father and I were sharing a few minutes of time about a rat in a wall eating wire. I now realize it was much more than that. It was a moment of bonding between a father and a very non-mechanical son, where a great unrealized love was found.

MY UNCLE THE DOG AND THE BURGLAR

Something that I find very strange is how the memory sometimes works. At the oddest times a memory from my childhood will seem to come out of nowhere. On these occasions, the recollection is so real that it is almost like I am reliving the event. This is the story of one of those memories.

When I was about seven or eight years old, we moved into a new house that was slightly larger and more isolated. It was exciting to me because, with all the trees and so much area to explore, it was almost like moving into the country. The only permanent residents living in the new house were me, my mom, my dad, my brother, and a great big collie named Beauty.

We had only lived in this home a very short time when we got our first visitor. It was my uncle, my mother's younger brother, who had been away at Army boot camp. Upon his return he had decided to spend a few days with us. I really didn't know my uncle very well, but that was about to change. Now remember, my uncle was just returning from completing his combat training. He had nerves of steel and in his mind his bravery was that of the superhero. At least that's how he saw himself.

As I look back upon this now, I recall my own training

and boot camp for the United States Marine Corps. You are trained so that your senses are razor sharp and you automatically react to situations with maximum effort, no matter how subtle the stimulus. For example, on my first visit home after training, my mother came into my room to wake me up. Immediately I jumped out of bed, came to attention, and yelled at the top of my voice, "All present and accounted for, sir, and ready for training!" This startled my mother so badly she almost fell backwards down the steps.

Maybe this will help the reader understand why my uncle reacted the way he did to the situation I am about to describe.

My uncle arrived at our house shortly after dinner, and for the next couple hours he regaled us with tales of his experiences in the United States Army, however limited those experiences might have been. He said his training had honed his body into a deadly weapon that would allow him to face any situation and come out the victor. Little did we know that this "weapon" was about to be tested severely and in a most unexpected way.

I guess it was around 9:30 or 10 o'clock that evening when my uncle finally went to bed. He said it was going to be the first good night sleep he had had in weeks, and he intended to take advantage of every second of it. I'm sure he fell almost instantly into a very deep, restful sleep. As you know, when you're awakened from a slumber, it takes a little while to get your bearings about where you are or what you're doing, even when you're in familiar settings. But when you have just left the pressure of Army boot camp and you're in a strange new house for the first time, it's easy to get confused.

So after my uncle had gone to bed, and without his knowledge, my father went outside and allowed Beauty to sleep in the kitchen and have the freedom to roam

13

downstairs, as was her habit every night. The dog's claws would click and scratch on the polished wooden floors as she would walk from room to room. Everyone in the house was already used to this, though, and therefore they paid no mind to it. Everyone that is, except for my uncle.

Now I'm not sure if he was awakened by the sound of Beauty roaming around downstairs or because nature had called, but in his drowsiness he heard the clicking and scratching sounds coming from downstairs and was compelled to investigate the source.

I guess his army training had somehow become instinctual at this point, because after briefly assessing the situation, he came to the conclusion that the source of the noise might be some hostile demonic force. And, of course, it had to be dealt with. My uncle, being the good soldier that he was, armed himself with a flashlight and a pistol (which, unbeknownst to him, fired blanks), which he found in his nightstand drawer. Thus armed he got into stealth mode and set off to investigate the mysterious sound.

Slowly he crept out of his room and made his way down the hall. When he reached the top of the stairs, he took them one at a time, moving as softly and as quietly as possible. As he neared the bottom of the stairs, he realized that the sound was coming from the room directly to the left, which would've been our kitchen. When he reached the second step from the bottom he crouched down in order to make his body as little a target as possible. Then he proceeded down the final step.

Just then the board underneath this foot creaked slightly, and instantly the noise coming from the kitchen ceased. Feeling that he might have been detected, his nerves were now all on edge and his imagination was running wild. Instinctively he held his breath. Large beads of sweat covered

14

his forehead and his legs began to shake. This is a well-known scientific and medical condition known as "being terrified."

In his present state of mind, the only conclusion he could possibly reach was that a burglar was in the kitchen. It was up to him to apprehend this night thief and thus become a hero, not only to our family, but to the entire community at large. He might even get a citation from the Army!

So, as slowly as he could in the inky darkness, he poked his head around the corner of the door frame to get a better look of the kitchen. What he could not possibly have known was that the dog, being alerted by the squeaking of the step, had also decided to investigate the source of the sound. She was just on the other side of the doorframe in a crouched position, ready to strike.

So, in the complete darkness of the house, as my uncle's head turned the corner of the kitchen, his nose bumped right into the cold, wet nose of our beloved collie, Beauty.

First, my uncle screamed in the face of what he perceived as a furry-faced monster. Then, all at once, he turned on the flashlight, pulled the trigger on the blank pistol, and began to wet his pants. (So much for bravery.) The dog didn't do much better. After barking in my uncle's face, she took off across the kitchen, slipping and sliding and peeing the entire way, before finding refuge in the corner, where she proceeded to bark, howl, growl and shake all at the same time.

My uncle, believing that he had just come face-to-face with a monster, fell back against the steps, his hand clutching his chest. At the time he thought he was having a massive heart attack, but it turned out to be just panic. He was hyperventilating as if he had just finished three marathons. In his mind, the head of whatever was connected to that cold, wet nose was growing exponentially by the second.

My father and mother, who were asleep in the bedroom at the end of the long hallway, had been enjoying the bliss of slumber when they were suddenly awakened by the blast of the blank pistol. My father, being unfamiliar with the new bedroom, instinctually tried to run out into the hall to find the source of the explosion. But in his confusion he chose the wrong door and ran directly into his closet, pulling the door closed behind him. Now trapped and in utter darkness, he spun around violently to try and find a way out and ended up getting wrapped up in all of the clothes. My mother had fallen out of bed at the sound of the blast was now sitting on the floor screaming in terror.

Eventually breaking out of the closet, my father, now with most of his wardrobe wrapped around his body, tripped over my panic-stricken mother and hit his head on the bedroom door, knocking out the bottom panel sending him into an even greater state of confusion.

This entire chaotic episode, from start to finish, occurred in less than 30 seconds.

By this time I too was awake and seem to have been the only person in the house with enough common sense to turn on a light. Looking down the hallway and turning to my left, I instantly noticed a hole in the bottom of my parents' bedroom door. I then proceeded to the edge of the steps, where I saw my uncle at the bottom in the throes of what he believed to be a fatal heart attack. My concern, of course, was for my beloved Beauty. I quickly descended the stairs and entered the kitchen. Turning on the light, I saw her crouched in the corner and I ran over to comfort her.

With the lights on and everybody back in the rational world, it didn't take long for us all to figure out what had happened. Once the initial fear and panic wore off, we began to laugh at the ridiculousness of it all, knowing that this was going to be a story we'd be retelling time and time again.

And that, my friends, is the true story of my uncle, the collie, and the burglar.

MY FATHER'S HAND

One of my earliest childhood memories is of me sitting in a chair beside my father while he tells me about what he thought and how he felt on the day I was born. I remember this story so well because I asked him to tell me about it again and again. I can still recall looking up at his weathered face, all full of lines and crags. But what struck me most were his eyes. When he told me the story, his eyes were once again full of life and youth.

The one thing that really sticks with me is what he told me he did the first time he approached me in the hospital room. He said I was so little and fragile that he thought I might break if he touched me too hard. Very slowly, he extended his worn and calloused finger to me, and immediately I grasped it in my tiny hand. It was one of the few times in my life that my father ever admitted to anyone that he had actually cried.

As I grew older and my relationship with my father changed, again and again I would recall that image of my hand around his finger, and no matter what was going on, it suddenly didn't seem all that important.

Throughout my life, I was always struck by my dad's hands. They had great character. They were strong and muscled from all the years he worked so hard to support his family. It didn't matter if he was sick or hurt; my father always went to work because he said he had a sacred responsibility to provide for his family. He also believed that if you worked for a man, you gave him an honest day's work for an honest day's pay. People who heard him say this called him old fashioned. To me, however, he was just telling the truth, as he had always done as my father. And he taught and expected me to do the same.

As I grew older, I also grew out of the kissing-my-father stage and chose instead to shake his hand, which was to me was more manly (How silly was I?). Gradually, as time passed, I also noticed a marked change in his hands – the same ones that had lifted me up when I needed it and disciplined me when I deserved it. They had become less firm and less defined as the years went by. Then they began to shake a little, and for the first time in his life, my father began to complain about the aches and pain in them. But he still never went to see the doctors, whom he never trusted.

As we grew older, and I began to realize that my father was not invincible, I saw him begin to grow weak and feeble, and I couldn't understand what was happening to us. Toward the end, he no longer talked of me but of himself and my mom. Then the day came when he saw that I had become a man worthy of his deepest trust. He told me what he wanted me to do at the end of his life.

I didn't want to hear these words because deep down I believed that to speak them would somehow make them come true. I was foolish enough to believe that if we were silent about the matter it would never happen. But eventually, I realized I had to hear his words and obey his wishes. He made me the executor of his will because he knew I would always have the courage to carry out his wishes, no matter how painful they were to me. Finally, that dreaded day arrived. It was a bright Wednesday, and I thought how different that completion of the day didn't match the completion of what I was feeling. Thankfully, God was merciful, and my father slipped into a gentle coma after only one day. I knew it wouldn't last long.

When I realized that the end was near, my mom and I moved to his bedside – she on his left, me on his right. For all of my education, military experience, and life wisdom, I still felt awkward because I didn't know what the right thing to do was.

What happened next is why I LOVE God so much.

As I bent down to talk to my father, touch his cheek, and tell him it was okay to die, unconsciously, I put my finger in the palm of his hand. And with what little strength he had left, my father squeezed my finger.

A flood of memories washed over me, but the one that I focused on was my father's story about the day I was born. Overwhelmed with love and grace, I suddenly realized we had come full circle. My dad was there when I was born into this human life, and now I was there as he was being born into his eternal LIFE, his eternal GLORY, and his eternal LOVE. It was then that I began to weep - not because of what I was about to lose, but because, for one of the first times in my life, I could pray a pure prayer of gratitude to my God for making me understand that in loving Him what I could never lose. I was never more grateful to God for allowing me to be a Christian.

As my father's breathing grew shallow, and as he began to slip away, I again became aware of a profound change in the features of his face. Suddenly, he relaxed, and the years began to melt away. The toil and strain were leaving. As he became less and less of what I had always known him to be, I suddenly realized what Christ meant when He said: When you do it to the least, you also do it to me.

My heart was hurting and bursting with love at the same time. I felt both joy and sorrow, and I would not have traded that moment for any amount of riches on this Earth. My father was becoming what was promised to all of us who believe in God: He was becoming one with Christ.

Then his heart stopped, and he let out his final breath. What I thought would come in an explosion of pain, came in a whisper of joy and love.

It would be a lie if I said I didn't miss my father. I wish he was still here to tell me, once again, about the day I was born. Funny, but that sensation only lasts but a moment, and then I remember, at the end, his finger in my hand, his rebirth into Paradise, and I can only smile and cry just a little. This is how we all wish to end - with the one's we love going to those that love us most.

Just a little end note: By the way, Dad, I just wanted you to know that I am taking good care of Mom. Don't worry: We will all be together again.

I love and miss you, Dad.

Your son,
Richard

THE STORY OF MY LITTLE WHITE DOG

I have always believed that the lessons we are taught by nature seem to be the simplest in form and the most complex in content. Nature has the ability to show us in a few well-chosen moments what would take many textbooks and years of study to produce in an academic-only atmosphere, and even then may never succeed. The spirit of nature seems to know and understand that human beings learn the fastest when they see and feel the lesson. Maybe schools and churches should sit back and rethink their means of presenting the materials that they think are so important. Maybe the lesson should aim to touch the heart first, before the intellect.

Let me give you one example of what I am trying to say. Animals have played a great role in my life. I can't remember a time when I didn't have a dog or cat in my house. There were also rabbits, turtles, hamsters, and even little shrimp bought from the back of a comic book store, without mom's permission, but mine just the same. Having these pets taught me responsibility, respect, joy, and comfort. I tried to look beyond the simplicity of Nature's teaching.

The one pet that is foremost in my mind is one little white dog named Pipkin. She was a total accident because she was the last little puppy in a litter from a Maltese mother named Pooka. This little mother had given birth to three puppies over the course of 12 hours, and we all thought that she was finished. Then, lo and behold, she slowly made her way over to me and began to softly whimper, signaling one more birth.

It didn't take long at all before puppy number four was born and came into my world. Little did I know that I would never be the same after this event. The newborn puppy was smaller than a mouse and was not breathing. She was blue and cold, and I thought she had been born dead. But I had yet to learn how powerful the spirit of life was in the heart and soul of that tiny creature.

I picked her up and gently began to rub her with a warm towel and blow into her little pink nose. The mother sat there looking up at me, as if to say, please, don't give up, do all you can to save my littlest child. Looking down into those little black pleading eyes, I knew I would not give up.

Then, a miracle. The little form began to stir, and the faintest whimper came out of her mouth. Reaching down, I presented her to her mother, who knew what to do from there. She began to softly and gently caress her newest offspring until that little ember of heat and light, showing the evidence of life, had been fanned into a bright flame, and Pipkin was finally with her three much bigger brothers.

From the very beginning of her life, Pipkin showed that one's size doesn't really matter that much in this world. It is the size of the heart and spirit that makes all the difference.

No matter how many times these much bigger puppies pushed her away, Pipkin fought back to her mother and got her rightful share of food and love. She began to grow but was always minuscule compared to other dogs. When she was grown, she was just a little handful of fur with four legs, two tiny black eyes, one black button nose and the heart of a lion. She never realized how small she was. It didn't matter to her if it was the giant of a postman or the elephant of the neighbor's dog; they were not coming into her domain without her permission. Many times I arrived just at the last moment to rescue her from being swallowed by a cat or carried off by a large hawk. But still, even at these dangerous times, she would never back down.

The thing that I remember most about her heart was not just her lack of fear or her great power to give what seemed like endless energy, but how much she could love me. Whenever I would pick her up, she needed to show me that she understood those first few seconds of life and what I had done. More important, she would always show what it meant to her. She loved me with her whole spirit because I gave her a chance to live and become herself. I was never able to discipline her (not that she ever needed it) because her answer to anything I ever did or how stern my voice was to bestow on my hand many soft and gentle kisses. She would slowly work her way to my cheek. By that time I had forgotten what she had done, and I would softly stroke her head and ears and rub her little chest. I would hold her close to me and love her deeply, simple, purely.

It is an interesting fact of life that when we are in love or love something, we are never aware of the finality of what we have or are doing. We just seem to enjoy the time, and we are shielded by our joy and love from any thoughts that the situation will ever change or end. I was this way with Pipkin. The thought never entered my mind that the seeds of her death were sown in her size. Although she had a great heart and spirit, her tiny body was frail and somewhat weak; that her ability to fight off disease had been very much compromised and that cancer was already eating its way through that little body and would end her beautiful life, all too soon.

Even now as I write these words, many years later, my tears are freely falling onto this page as I type the story of my gentle and loving little friend. I can still see her standing there looking at me with those two twinkling little eyes asking me to pick her up just one more time and hold her close to my heart, gently and softly patting her little head. What I wouldn't give for one of those little kisses that are so fresh in my heart as I touch my cheek and cry.

I began to notice that something was very wrong when it was already too late to do anything to stop the situation. My little dog had cancer in her brain and there was nothing I could do to help her when she looked into my eyes for understanding and comfort. The only blessing was that there was no pain in her condition. But it seemed that the more her body failed, the more her love increased. When she could no longer hold her head up, I would sit and rock her in my arms humming sweetly and out would come her little tongue, and she would softly touch my arm. She would look up, I would touch her head, and she would soon fall asleep, and I could almost believe I saw her smiling up at me.

Finally, on the last day, she could no longer open her eyes and her breaths were short and in little pants. I placed her on the bed between my wife and myself and holding her gently told her it was alright to leave us. Then with one last little effort she drew in her last breath and was gone. Her little head turned slightly and for the last time rested on my arm. It ended where it had begun, in my hands.

I wrapped her in a blanket with her favorite toy and buried her in the little garden under my front window where I could see her always. I planted many flowers there and every spring and summer I see her beautiful spirit in the glory of their colors.

The story of this little dog does not end at her death but it begins there. As I stated when I began this story I now have to tell you what nature taught me by this smallest of souls.

As I now look back on her time in my life, all that I want to do is to love all others and especially my GOD as this little dog loves me. I never want to remember that they made me angry, hurt my feelings, and slighted my ego. I don't want my first reaction to be to strike back at all who offend me or wrong me. I want my first reaction to be to gently kiss their hand and by the time I get to their cheek forget what made me angry and to only enjoy the love of the moment.

When it is my time to die I want my GOD to gently put me on HIS bed close beside His chest and to stroke my head gently and tell me it is OK to come to HIM because no matter what I did, HE still loves me. And when I am gone I want Him to plant me in HIS garden If Love and let every flower that booms above me give testament to His great love for me and humble love in return. I want to love as I was loved by this little dog. I want to be thankful for the Hands that brought me into this world, protected me and touched my heart while I was here and then gently carried me home when it is my time to leave.

As I stated when I began, "Nature is the greatest teacher." In spite of all of my formal education, great readings and diligent study, after all of my academic honors and degrees my greatest lesson in life was taught to me by a little dog with the biggest heart I have ever felt and the greatest spirit I have ever known. In this world that seems so harsh and cold at times, there can be found in the simplest of places pure love and grace if we know where to look or would just let it happen to us.

I can only hope and pray that, at the end of my life, I have finally become worthy of the great gift and lesson in love that was my little white dog, Pipkin.

BEN BREEDLOVE'S STORY: A LIFE, A FAITH A TRIBUTE

"A Butterfly Counts Not Months But Moments and He Has Time Enough"

It's amazing nowadays how through the power of social media you can not only meet and become friends with total strangers from all over the world, but you can also actually come to know and love them. Such was the case with Ben Breedlove. I felt compelled to write the following tribute because of how this remarkable young man touched my heart and taught me about faith, life, and love. He must never be forgotten. If you have never heard of this remarkable young man, please look him up on YouTube and watch *"This Is My Story"*, Part One and Part Two.

Ben Breedlove lived in Austin, Texas, and was born with a congenital heart disease. On Christmas Day 2011, Ben passed away as a result of this heart condition. He was just 18 years old. He made the two above mentioned videos on December 18 of that year telling of his life and an extraordinary experience. This was only one week before his death. These two videos have been viewed by over 12 million people (and counting). The people who have watched these videos post comments on how they have changed their hearts, faith, and their lives.

People in this world must come to realize that we do *not* see with God's eyes; our knowledge is not God's knowledge; our power is not God's power. From a medical or scientific standpoint, Ben's heart was broken because it was imperfect, or unusable. But this is not what God said. He said, "Ben, come stand with Me in "Your Faith", because I wish to show the people of the world what I can do with that heart that medicine and science say is of no use." Ben, in his great faith said, "Yes, Father!"

For most of his life, Ben couldn't play team sports, and he wasn't able to do what other young men his age could do. Instead of feeling sorry for himself and blaming God and the world for his condition, he just enjoyed everything that he could do and lived a grace-filled and loving life to its absolute fullest. Again, here is where God sees things so much differently than we do. God said, "Okay Ben, then you will play on My team, where it's the *DEPTH* of your *heart*, not its *CONDITION*, that makes all the difference." Again Ben in faith answered, "Yes, I'll play."

Now the interesting thing is that on God's team you only play one game and it's called *HEARTS*. It is played like this: You have a given amount of time known only to God. In that amount of time you have to run as fast as you can through your life and collect as many hearts as you can for God before you cross the finish line. Ben understood this game beyond human knowledge; for as soon as God asked him to run, Ben took off and never looked back. When he crossed the finish line on Christmas Day 2011, Ben had collected over 1 million hearts. But the interesting thing about this game is that when Ben crossed the line, his Game did not *end;* rather, it was just *beginning.*

Had Ben been born with what human beings and science considers to be a perfect heart, and something had happened to him and he chose to donate that heart to someone else, he may have only affected a few people. But God took that imperfect heart, combined it with His love and grace, and showed us what can be done with something that appears broken in the eyes of men.

In God's game of *HEARTS,* it is not up to the player to determine if the hearts collected are acceptable to God or if God might not be able to use them. The player's job is just to collect the hearts. Christians sometimes get their job description and responsibilities mixed up. The Christian's job is to cast the net. It is God's responsibility to sort the fish.

Sometimes we want to do God's job. We want to say this heart, this person, this soul isn't worth collecting because God won't want or be able to use them. How foolish we are. Ben, on the other hand, played the game to perfection and now you can count the hearts he collected and is *still* collecting. Count the number of lives he changed because he let God do the sorting.

Unlike the games of men, anyone and everyone can play God's game of *HEARTS.* All that we have to do is go to and love God, have faith and agree to be on his team and play by His rules.

Many people without faith have asked me why God would take this young man from his family, church, school, his community, where he was loved and cherished by everyone. Why would God make this child be born with a diseased heart where he would be limited his whole life? They are very surprised by my answer. God did it in this way, I tell them, because He *loved* Ben!

When we become Christians we don't just join a club.

We must become new people, new creatures in Christ. We agreed to deny God nothing He would ever ask from us or of us. The symbol of our faith is not a cross without purpose. Christ didn't say take up your car, your home, business, family, friends, sports, or even your heart and follow me. Instead, He said to take up your *cross* – your particular burden or challenge – and follow me. In this contract God never asks for more than he is willing to compensate us.

God asked this family, those friends, that church, that school, that community, to let Ben return to Him. In Ben's earthly place, God left His grace, comfort, love, and His presence. Ben is not gone; he lives in the heart and spirit of every person he ever knew or had contact with and knew him, whether in person or through his YouTube videos. If you want to be with Ben again, all that you have to do is to come together in a true spirit of faith and love as God told us, and Ben is once more among us. "For where two or more gather in my name, I am with them." (Matthew 18:20)

Peter Marshall, the great preacher, once said, "If the departed are with Christ and Christ is with us, then they are never far away."

There are some creatures and souls in God's kingdom that are not destined to grow old. Ben was one of these. He was here to teach us a special lesson with his life that must be taught in a very short and intense time: how to love and be loved. His life makes people understand that no matter what their condition, weakness, or position in life, they can be better than they ever thought they could be. It only takes a faith and love in God. He revealed our potential for good in a very special way. This was obviously a very special grace from God: Ben was that grace.

Again, in the eyes of men what looks to be a tragedy is a triumph for God. What looks to be defeat becomes victory with God! And it is a triumph for Ben and our family to see that his life was a life well-lived!

You know it might be hard to believe there is a second part to this remarkable young man's story. On December 6, 2011, Ben was walking in his school when he realized he was about to faint. He sat on a bench and passed out. When he awoke, the EMTs were working on him and he heard them say that he had no pulse and no respiration for about three minutes. They were about to try to shock his heart back into action. He could not talk or move, but he knew he was awake, and that this experience was not a dream. When they said "Go!" and were about to shock his heart, he blacked out again.

Ben then tells of entering a long, endless white room with no walls that was lit by warm, bright light. He was dressed in a beautiful suit and was standing in front of the mirror. When he looked into the mirror at his reflection, he remarked how good he looked and how proud he was of everything that he had done in his life and how he couldn't stop smiling. He said it was the greatest feeling of peace and joy he had ever felt.

He goes on to tell of meeting his favorite recording artist there, Kid Cudi. They began talking about his favorite song, "Mr. Rager", and when they got to part where it says "When will the fantasy end? When will the heaven begin?", Kid Cudi said, "Go now." Then Ben came back to consciousness as the EMTs were administering CPR on him.

He told them that he did not want to come back. He never wanted to leave that place and that feeling of peace. Then he asked them the most remarkable question. "Do you believe in God and angels?" he asked. But before they could answer, he exclaimed, "I do!"

In the New Testament epistles, there is a line in first Corinthians that I've always wondered about: *"What I see now is but a dim image in a mirror when that which is perfect comes that which is imperfect passes away."* (1 Corinthians 13:12) Having a background in both theology and philosophy, I've often thought St. Paul put this line in because he was talking to the Greeks. He was comparing Christ to the Platonic idea of this being an imperfect world, and that there was another perfect place, so the Greeks might more easily understand and relate to what he was trying to tell them about heaven. For the Greeks understood *perfection* much better than they understood the concept of *goodness*.

For me it wasn't Ben speaking; it was the spirit of God speaking through Ben's experience. God was saying that at some point in time each and every one of us will be standing before that mirror. When our time comes, will we like what we see and be proud of what we did with our life? We believe it is when we will see ourselves the way God sees us – not through a veil but as His creation – in the state of how He meant for us to be!

In this earthly light we may see ourselves, our accomplishments, our material possessions, and our lifestyle and think we are ready to stand in that perfected light in front of that Divine mirror. But are we?

This awesome young man has shown us by his life and story that all of our worldly deeds, accomplishments, and possessions might serve to show that we have lived larger than life. This young man's humble acceptance of God's will, law, faith, and love in his life, and then living that life in love, faith, and service to others shows that he lived a life that was larger than *death*.

On Christmas Day of 2011, when Ben Breedlove crossed the line in the game of *HEARTS,* he fell into his loving Savior's arms. I am sure that Jesus looked down upon this remarkable soul and said, "Well done, my good and faithful servant." Ben now sits with Christ, bearing that ever-present smile on his face and wearing that great looking suit as he waits for us.

God used Ben to show each of us how to play this game, what the rules are, and how to win for Him. It is now for each of us to say "Yes", move to God's team, and start running. For each of us that line is a different length. For Ben it was 18 years; for others it may be a 118 years. But one thing is for certain: It is a game each of us *can* win, and it is the *best* game in town.

If there is a final lesson we can learn from Ben's remarkable life it is this: when our life is over and it is time for us to leave this earth, we should have lived in such *faith* and *love* that we are remembered not for the hole we leave when we are gone but for the light we gave while we were here!

"When will the fantasy end? When will the heaven begin?"

Go now.

Do you believe in God and angels? "*I DO!*"

THE WISH

Once, a long time ago, there was a beautiful green valley nestled between very high, steep, snow-covered mountains. There was a village in this lush valley where a great treasure could be found. But this was no ordinary treasure of silver or gold or precious stones. The great treasure of this valley was a little orphaned boy.

Every family in the village had helped raise him, and each loved him as their own child. Although he was an orphan, he was never sad because he had so many mothers and fathers and brothers and sisters. But this was no ordinary little boy, for this gentle child had a magnificent gift: No matter where he went or who he saw, he brought great love, joy, and happiness to everyone and everything he touched.

From the time when the little boy first learned to walk and to talk, he said that he had only one wish: When he was old enough and strong enough, he wanted to travel beyond his beloved mountains. He believed that there were other worlds and great and beautiful things to see. But he always said that when the time came that he was finished seeing the world beyond the mountains, he would return home and live the rest of his life in his beautiful village and love all of the people that had loved him. This always brought great joy to the hearts of the people.

But just after his 8th birthday, he began to grow ill and very weak. Everyone in the village was sad beyond measure because they knew he would not be with them much longer. But what made them sadder still was that the weaker he got the more desperate was his wish to know and visit the world beyond the mountains.

The whole village was beside itself trying to figure out how to grant this last wish of the child that they loved so much. They knew that he would never survive leaving his house let alone crossing the mountains. They saw for the first time in his life the little boy was sad for he knew how sick he was.

One day a stranger came to the village on his way to another country and stopped at the inn for some food and rest. He couldn't help but notice how sad everyone was and asked why. So they told him the sad tale of the little boy and his unfulfilled wish.

To their astonishment and delight, the stranger asked if he could meet the little boy. This made the villagers happy. They knew that the little boy loved talking to all of the strangers that came to the village and asking them to tell stories about the places and things beyond his mountains.

So they took the stranger to the little boy's room. When the little boy saw the stranger, he smiled for the first time in weeks and began to ask him all kinds of questions. But the man did not answer him. Instead he asked the little boy about his wish.

The little boy answered the old man with deep sadness in his voice. When the boy finished speaking, the stranger said something unbelievable. He told the boy that he had the power to grant the wish within three months. For the first time in many weeks happiness came back into the little boy's eyes.

All the villagers had quite a different reaction to what the stranger had said. And as soon as he left the house, they showed their anger. "How could you be so cruel and give that dear child such a false hope?" they said. But the man replied that he *did* have the power to grant the wish. They asked if he was a great wizard.

"No, I am not a wizard," he replied.

"Then are you one of God's powerful angels?" they asked.

Again he replied, "No. I am not an angel."

Still, they pressed him further. "Are you a living saint then?"

Once again, his answer was no. He told them that if they would just be a little patient they would see for themselves that he did really possess the power to grant the little boy's wish. None of the villagers believed him, but there was little that they could do but wait and see what happened.

For the next three months the stranger visited the little boy every day, and, as he had promised, after three months he had fulfilled the wish. The little boy could go beyond his mountains no matter how sick or weak he became.

You may by wondering how this stranger had such a power to perform this miracle. After all, as the man said, he was not a wizard, he was not an angel, and he was not a saint.

He was a teacher, and he taught the little boy to read! When you can read the World comes to you.

THE FOOTBALL HERO

"Touchdown!" blares the voice over the public address system. "With that pass, Wade Williams becomes the leading passer in Ashley High School history!"

The people in the stands go wild. Wade is mobbed by his teammates. The tall blond player doesn't even feel the steady rain pelting down on him this cold October night. He can only feel that set of eyes focused on his back and, with a sideways glance, he can see him sitting there all alone in his usual section of the stands.

All of the kids refer to him as "the retard," the weird kid that nobody knows because he goes to that special school across town. No one has ever figured out why he comes to every home game because he doesn't seem to know anybody or understand anything that is going on. Some kids say he just likes to watch the movement. For the last four years he has been mocked and insulted, but he just doesn't seem to understand anything.

Wade is given the game ball by the coach, who then pats him on the back for being a real hero, both to his team and his school. But it is as if the football player has gone deaf. He can hear nothing. He can only see that little boy sitting all alone in the rain.

What should have been Wade's greatest moment of pride was his greatest moment of shame. Suddenly he realizes that he has to make things right and that, for the first time in his life, he doesn't care what other people might think or say. He doesn't care about his reputation. He must tell the truth. For the first time he has the courage to let his secret go. He bolts from the cheering crowd and jumps the fence and sprints to where the little boy is sitting. The crowd and his teammates are stunned.

Wade puts his hand on the little boy's shoulder, bends over, and gives the boy a gentle kiss on the head. Then he holds the game ball out and says, through his tears, "This is for you, little brother!"

The little boy takes the ball. Then he reaches out, takes his big brother's hand, and holds it to the side of his face as his tears flow over his brother's fingers. He does understand, after all.

Long after the cheering stops, long after all of the people and the players have left the field trying to come to terms with what has just happened, late into the wet and cold night, two figures sit in an empty stadium holding each other but saying nothing. These two lone figures are the living definition of winning. They show that victory has nothing to do with playing fields or battlefields. They show that heroes aren't the people who run the fastest or who can play the best. The greatest victories and the greatest heroes in this world are those who can find the courage and grace to do what is right out of the power of love and not gain.

These two people sitting alone in the rain are a living testimony to the fact that it is never too late to love. They are a monument to the victory that is the power of love.

UNDERSTANDING THE IRISHMAN

I think it is interesting that many people who are not Irish have difficulty understanding those who are. To them the Irishman seems to have a confusing nature and a changeability that is unsettling to the non-Celt. If you really want to understand an Irishman, what you must know is that within his chest beats five different hearts. Not a five-chambered heart but five individual hearts at the same time. At any given moment one or more of these hearts is in control.

First, in the chest of every Irishman, is the heart of the King. He sees himself as anointed by God as a lawgiver, a dispenser of justice, a protector of his people who is worthy to sit upon the throne.

Second is the heart of a warrior. He sees himself as a knight seated upon a valiant charger, ready to right wrongs, protect the weak, guard the innocent, dispense justice, do battle with evil, and triumph always for the good.

Third is the heart of saint. The Irishman tries with all of his might to do God's will, but most of the time he winds up doing his will in God's name. He feels he has great faith, and yet he is not religious. When he prays he feels God is listening directly and only to his voice, and that He will grant his petitions and wishes. When God doesn't, the Irishman feels it will only be a matter of time before the Almighty changes his mind because, of course, God is Irish.

Fourth, in the chest of every Irishman, beats the heart of the devil. He knows that he should be good, but he realizes that evil is much more fun. He doesn't try to be malicious or mean; things just seem to work out that way. He tries with all of his might to be good but realizes his own human weakness and frailty. And after giving in to temptation, he resolves always to do better next time, knowing that this may never be the truth, but the promise is still made.

Last, and most important, there is the heart of the poet. For every Irishman is a man of words. He is able to motivate, to inspire, to move, to motivate, to lift up, to tear down, to pass on, and to ennoble by the words he uses. The words seldom originate in his head but more often flow to his mouth from his heart. They are the essence of whom and what he is, where he came from, and where he longs to go. They are his vision of how life should be, of how the world should work, and of how people should act toward one another. It is as if God is whispering his great plan for mankind in the ear of the Irishman, and it is his duty to change the world with his words. He is the custodian of his nation's history and culture. He is the teller of stories; the poet of his nation. Above all others he knows that words not only have meaning but also power, and this power has been entrusted to the Irish more than to anyone else on earth.

So, the next time you're in contact with and Irishman, and you are confused about his nature, listen for a moment and find out which heart is speaking. His words his actions and his emotions will help you understand that he is longing to leave his mark in the hearts, minds, and souls of all that he meets.

CATHEDRALS AND CASTLES

I have been very lucky in my life to have done a great deal of traveling, especially in Europe. In college I had been a European history major, with a great love for the time period known as the "Middle Ages." I had also taught history for two years before going on an adventure to the continent, which was to become one of the greatest thrills of my life. I wanted to go to all of the places I'd read about and to touch the very graves of the people whom I had never met, but who were so very real to me.

In my approach to history, I try not to judge people for their actions, but rather to try to understand what it was in their minds, hearts, and souls that made them act the way they did. Intellectually, I try to put myself back in their time to see if I would have made the same choices. There is a German word coined by Goethe, the renowned writer of Faust. That word is "zeitgeist," which literally means a "time spirit" or "time ghost." This means to try and recreate the spirit of the time that is being studied by going back to the source documents and trying to get an understanding of what was important in their lives, what was their world view. How did they see themselves and the world in which they lived?

Eventually, I abandoned this scholarly approach,

because the more I traveled I found that books were not needed to accomplish my task; everywhere I went, in every country I visited, the people had left the answer to all my questions not in books but in buildings – in their castles and cathedrals.

A castle was built as a symbol of great worldly power. It was meant to cast a shadow of fear over all within its sight. It was built to be so imposing that an enemy would give up trying to attack because it would be too costly in lives and in resources, even if the attack were successful. The castle speaks of order maintained by force of arms, birth, oath, and pain. Everyone understood that the owner of the castle was someone not to be trifled with. Everyone knew their place and knew that they could never change it. The castle said be very afraid, and don't even think about change. Castles were constructed out of fear as well, a fear of losing your worldly possessions. Common people lived and died within sight of its walls, without ever seeing another place.

Then there were the cathedrals. These structures serve almost exactly the same function as castles but in a spiritual sense. They were built to protect the souls of the builders and much more. When you stand at the steps and look around, you can't distinguish where the cathedral ends and heaven begins. This is not an accident. These people were able to express in stone what they felt in their hearts and believed in their souls. This building for them was a physical prayer, it expressed with great eloquence the way they saw themselves, who they were, what they were, and, more important, how they saw their relationship with God.

They tried to make a place that was so beautiful that when God was there, He wouldn't miss Heaven. It was so immense that when the individual entered the great edifice they were humbled but not afraid. They could feel the protective arms of God wrap around them and say, "Don't worry, I will save you." The further they walked into the shrine, the smaller they got, and the more they had to rely on something much larger than themselves.

These people built their prayers in stone. They expressed their faith, hopes, dreams, wishes, and most of their love for their Creator and His plan for their lives using their hands like the Father did when he created them. He reached to touch them and gave them life, and they were reaching back to say, "Thank you."

These churches weren't built in decades like castles; they were built in lifetimes. The people who began these projects knew that they would never live to see them finished. But that didn't matter to them. They were expressing eternity. Their lifetime didn't matter; the house of God among them did. These people, who were the most poor, were leaving the greatest treasure that they could for those that followed them. What they lacked in material wealth they made up for in grace, desire, and love.

At the end of my travels, I was awestruck that not one of the castles I visited was being used for the purpose for which it was constructed. They are now private homes, museums, or ruins. Yet each cathedral that still stands today is being used for the purpose for which it was built. These churches still have the power to humble and protect, and to lift the Spirit to elicit an unspoken prayer from the soul of any person that stands in that great space.

After all, I guess that the greatest proof of truth is time!

After many years of observation, study, and prayer, I now understand that we are in exactly the same place in history where these humble people once stood. We in our lifetime must make the same choices that they made. We must build our own castle or cathedral, not with stone and mortar but with the very actions of our lives. If we choose a life that causes fear in the weak and imposes our will on those around us, we impoverish the spirits of all with whom we have contact. But if we choose to build our lives as a living testament to our faith, our truth, and our love, we leave behind for those that follow a refuge from hate, oppression, fear, pain and poverty.

What will we build with our lives? Something to lift the soul or crush the spirit? Will we reach for more power, or will we reach for the hand of God to say, "Thank You, Father?" It is for each of us to decide. We must each find our own truth, faith, hope, desires, and, most important, love.

THE SINGER

"He Who Sings, Prays Twice" —St. Augustine

I think it is amazing that, most of the time, seemingly ordinary people don't realize how truly unique and gifted they really are. A great number of people in this world have hidden deep in their hearts, souls, and spirits, a secret that they believe is theirs alone: the desire to sing and to be recognized as a singer.

Little do these individuals know or understand how many others in this world share this hidden desire as well. Yet I believe few of these people will ever try to sing even one note in the presence of others because of a great fear they have that they will be laughed at, or that they do not possess the level of talent to sing well enough in public or to be accepted by that public. These poor souls need to realize two very small but important and fundamental facts: 1) God will never inspire a desire in your heart and soul and then deny you the Grace to fulfill that desire, if you but ask Him to fulfill it in faith and prayer with a humble heart and spirit; 2) Most people don't know what "to sing" really means.

Singing is not, as most people think, just the combined actions of making noise with your throat and sounds and tones with your lips. This is a narrow and shallow understanding of this great gift. If this definition was true, then everyone could sing (and we know that this idea just isn't true). To be a singer, you must not learn to write or to even try to sing your song first; you must learn to *live* your song first.

You must sing with the essence of your life that reflects the loving quality of your life. You must learn how to let the people listening to this most personal composition that is uniquely you, hear and feel the music that is God's love and grace on and inside your heart. They must see and then know the harmony that you try to maintain and reflect with all that you touch and all that touches you.

You must help them to understand what harmony really is by letting them see what you have done, not only in your life but also with the constancy of your life. Let this harmony tell of the most beautiful qualities of who you are, of the gentle touch of God upon your spirit. Let the breath of your song be of the same breath that God gave you at your own creation. Help others use your song to again find their way to God's light and love because they can see, feel, and understand His creative, life-restoring, and forgiving breath. Through your song, they can once again remember, with the greatest joy, why they live and why they exist: simply because they are loved by God their Father.

Offer to every person you meet this deep and most precious truth of your heart and soul. Help them to feel and hear the melody and rhythm of your very being in God. Let your high notes be the best and greatest that you know, feel, and believe. Let the low notes be the pain and suffering that you have known in your life, yet, with your Father's help and protection, you would not allow defeat you. With Faith in God you will never surrender to this weakness. Help them to

47

understand that each day of your life and theirs is a chance to add a new verse to your never-ending song of beauty, praise and love.

When you begin to live and understand this gift in its true power, light, and meaning, something amazing begins to happen. Those people listening to you who were deaf are able to hear you sing, and those people who were blind are now able to see what you are singing about. But most important of all, you will learn just how truly great a singer you can really be if you will but sing about the power of faith in God. If you will use this one small gift in the way that it was intended to be used and have faith in your Father's promise that you will be given His grace to succeed, then you will never fail.

Never sing for yourself; always dare to share your song with the world. Share your song not only because you have overcome, with God's help, your fear of singing in public, but sing now because you have found the true source of your courage and strength. Sing because you have found the awesome power of God's grace. You can now face your brothers and sisters with His music and song. Always allow your talent to flow gently from your heart first, and it becomes unnecessary to ever ask yourself that ridiculous question ever again: "Can I really sing"?

Because when you accept who you are, where you are, and what you are, you will finally understand that you have become a member of the chorus of God, whose sole purpose in existence is to praise Him, glorify Him, and reflect His love. It is to become one of the most beautiful singers in all of His creation and for all time.

So then, come with me, let us walk together with Him, hold His hand, and sing His songs. Let us learn together what it is really like to pray twice!

WHO IS MY GOD

All of my life I have had other people telling me about my God. Who He is and what He is like. Whom He loves and whom He hates. Whom He is for and whom He is against. I listened with polite silence and might have even believed these voices for a moment. But their God is not *my* God!

The Spirit who caresses my heart is not a being of temper or judgment. He is a father who teaches by example; who loves me without condition or status and asks only that I love back in the same degree and measure. That to love Him truly is to love and respect His creation and creatures, and to realize that all other people are my brothers and sisters in and by that love and not by their actions, faults, shortcomings, and sins.

His vision is clear and not clouded by anger. The way to Him is not complicated or confusing. All of the study about Him is worthless unless you first love Him, know Him, seek Him. He is hidden in plain sight.

To know my God is to know what it is to be childlike and not childish. It is to know that faith is not moving a mountain but rather throwing yourself back without looking, knowing you will land safely in His hands. It is to accept every day in faith and grace that the good, like the bad, is only temporary and will not destroy me.

To know my God is to hear his voice in the wind and the rain. It is to feel His touch in the warmth of the sun; to see his face in the heart and soul of every person I meet.

Many people will read these words and say this is not God. I must agree this is NOT their God. But I know what is in my heart and soul. I must follow His voice in the spirit that lights my way!

At the end of my life, when I finally see the truth of my belief, I pray that I find the God of my heart and not the God of my hearing!"

ON HUMAN LIFE

All human life is sacred. Life is also sacred at any point in its development and existence—to be born, alive, or ready to naturally end. No person has the right to terminate a life for any reason because no person has the power to create life. Life is a gift from a much higher power than man. Science, for all its wishful thinking, will never have the power to create life. It can put all the organic compounds known to man in all the glass dishes and test tubes in the world, and course every form of energy at any level through this material, and yet never will the result be life.

Science seems to be ignorant of one fact of nature: Life comes only from life. Life is an act of creation. Creation is the power to bring something into existence simply by thought and exercise of the will. Man or science will never have this power. If, then, man has not the power to create life, it follows that man does not have the right to destroy or end life at any time or by any means.

No human court or human system of justice, as flawed and imperfect as it has to admit that it is, can define when any human life begins, nor does it have the intelligence to determine when human life should cease or be terminated.

No words or ideas of men are ever higher than the basic right of life to exist and continue naturally to its conclusion.

There can never be a moral justification for abortion or capital punishment because no human idea, no form of human expression, has the power to negate this moral imperative. All legal precedents here must give way, for all legal systems deal only with the virtues of Justice or Mercy, and neither of these virtues is higher than the virtues of Love and Honor that is Life itself.

Capital punishment and abortion are no more than legally sanctioned human sacrifice upon the supposed high altar of Justice, while all the time keeping a blind eye to the higher altar of Mercy and the highest altars of Love and Honor. These blind actions only serve to make us that which we profess to hate and are trying to destroy! We then become death itself.

All of those people, enlightened by the Grace and Gift of God to know and understand this Truth, who stand in silence, stand also accused and convicted by that silence. Even though this watching crowd never wielded a scalpel in an abortion or moved a lever or pushed the syringe in an act of capital punishment, their very inaction empowered others to do these actions in their name, and they therefore stand as guilty and sinful as if they had acted personally in these crimes.

We as human beings have a collective Moral and Social responsibility to protect and value all life, if we expect individual life to have any value at all. Any action, whatsoever, that diminishes the value and merit of one single life diminishes the value and merit of all life. There is no such thing as good life or bad life—there is simply Life itself. Personal actions may be judged by society or its laws and morals to be good or bad, but the basic value of life itself is never changed or cheapened by these actions. Neither that basic humble respect for the gift that is life should ever be lost, nor the simple understanding of its value ever be compromised by financial necessity or social will.

LIGHT AND DARKNESS

In this world there are many different kinds of light—sunlight, moonlight, and starlight, to mention a few. What is unique about each of these is that they are all the enemies of darkness. Yet they all lack the power to vanquish the dark, for it still returns.

The only light that can conquer the darkness is the light that comes from love. When we are in love, we have no notion of the dark; there is no memory of groping blindly through life and only having our way lit by brief bursts of light, only to be thrust again into the darkness.

Love is its own light. When we love, we do not see with our eyes or hear with our ears; there is not tactile sense of touch; all our senses are directed by the heart, not the head. We are no longer one weak person but rather one with the power of two. Love has the ability to lead others so they no longer stumble and fall. The light of love never dims or dies, because once the flame is lit, darkness grows darker and it only serves to make the smallest light brighter.

The greatest of all love is that of God our Father for His children. In the beginning He gave us the sun to divide the darkness, and then He gave us the love of His Son to wipe it out forever.

THANKSGIVING IS ALSO A VERB

Thanksgiving is also a verb. Well, actually, it is really a gerund or gerundive, whichever you prefer. But let's not split grammatical hairs and lose the meaning of what I am trying to convey!

Thanksgiving is a blessing. A blessing can be given by anyone in any place at any time. This action means—at its most basic understanding—that we both realize and recognize that everything in our lives and even our very life itself is a gift. We are taking that instant of time and place to offer and show this awareness back to the source of all gifts, graces, and love: God.

To bless something is to respond to the insight of just how small and helpless we really are when left to our own devices and power. It is to know and internalize on a most basic level our true nothingness, our simplicity and our weakness. We are not ashamed or afraid of this state, but rather we rejoice and are grateful, faithful and loving because God has called us His children.

In this moment of humility and humanity, we are able to lift our eyes and hearts, and we can see and feel with our heart and spirit that all is gift, all is grace, and all is love; that no matter what we may have thought or felt in the past, we have no right or claim to anything. Yet, as God's children, we are given a new birthright to all that is His and all that He wills for us through His love: our everlasting life. We praise God that we are never alone or unloved, no matter what our earthly circumstances might be or appear to be.

The truest gift to our heart and soul is to know we will always have everything that we will ever need but never deserve. Because of the love of God, who is also our Father, we are given time and place, light and love, joy, and life. He asks only for our humble love in return and to recognize that all we will ever have comes from Him. He wants us to live in a state of constant Thanksgiving, both of and for Him and for each other.

GRACE: HOLY ENERGY FROM GOD

The very ability of a human being to become aware of a Divine concept such as grace is in itself an act of that very grace. Every person on earth actually exists in two different dimensions of being at the same time: the material world and the immaterial world.

In the material world we are condemned to definitions. Human beings will let nothing exist in the material world without a name. There is no object, substance, or matter in any form, either large or small, to which human beings don't attach a title. By simply assigning a sound to an object in order to identify it, human beings in some small way become the master of that object and, in turn, masters of the material world around them. We seem to feel that we become partners in its creation. How foolish we are to need such power that we would lay claim to a tiny part of an absolutely reserved Divine ability that we cannot even understand—the very act of creation itself.

The immaterial world, on the other hand, is the spiritual world. By this I don't mean spiritual simply in its religious meaning, but including that which seems to be invisible to us as well. We know that this world exists because we have attached titles to things. The concepts in this realm are called virtues. This special class of concepts is identified by the simple fact that when the virtue is mentioned there is not single object that comes to mind in the collective thought processes of all people. If I say the word *cat*, for example, everyone will bring to mind the same object: a four legged animal with fur, teeth, a tail, etc. It will not be the exact same image in everyone's mind, but it will still be a cat.

Similarly, with the idea of *virtue* there is no single symbol that will come to mind and be common to all hearers of the word. If I say the words *freedom*, *liberty*, *honor*, or *love*, each person will bring to his or her mind that object that for them is the symbol is that word.   Grace is such a word, such a virtue. Grace is not only the ability to recognize all that is beautiful in both worlds, it is the motion from God that allows us to participate in anything that is called beautiful. We think of our gifts and talents as abilities that we have somehow earned, and they place us about less gifted beings. The opposite is true. Grace is not a present; it isn't our possession in any way or form. It is a gentle call from the Creator to share with the rest of His Creation what He has whispered into our ears. It is a call to the noblest of vocations—that of service to the rest of creation.

The two powers of grace to work in and on our spirits and souls is first to call us to our given task in God's Creation that will complete and help to bring about all that He would have it and us become. Grace works in us first to be able to sing of the virtue and beauty that is Creation, and then it sanctifies us to become that virtue and beauty that is the Kingdom of God. If we are to become His children and the most beautiful part of all creation, we must know grace. Grace is the power that blends all that potential greatness and blessings within us and brings us together in a fraternal love and peace that reflects the smile of God.

MY TRIBUTE TO MY WIFE, MY LOVE, MY BEST FRIEND

Today was my 24th wedding anniversary, and as I sit here in the quiet evening, I reflect on those years. They were but a moment, a flash, an instant, and yet an entire lifetime. I can remember the time before, but I can't seem to feel it as I have in the more recent years. Love is funny that way. It is often said that the Irish and the Scots are tongue tied by love. Being an Irishman, I hope that words won't get in the way of what I really want to say.

One of the things that I find interesting is that, as I walked this earth for the first half of my life, alone, I thought that I possessed everything I would ever need to make me happy. I was strong and independent with a sense of purpose, which, at that period in time, seemed unerring. I was my own man and needed only my own gifts and talents to be forever content, peaceful, and successful. My friends and family had given up on the idea that marriage was ever in my future and had even collected their bets as each year passed.

I wasn't looking for someone to share what I had and had become, because, without realizing it, I was very selfish in the name of an accomplished person. There were many girls and then, in later life, ladies with whom I was willing to share moments of my life. But I was never willing or desirous to share my entire life.

Isn't it funny how God is so subtle and wise? I had no idea I was even looking for someone until I walked into a room one day and saw a pair of eyes that stopped me in mid-sentence and mid-step. I had been all over the world; I had seen oceans and islands, mountains and valleys, sunrises and sunsets, and I thought that these experiences defined what was most beautiful in my world. But those eyes seemed to burn into my very soul and spirit, and all that I had known as beautiful was no longer fresh but pale and obscured by some invisible fabric that I could neither see nor touch. The only clear thing in my life at that moment was those soft and inviting eyes. They weren't even looking at me, but I could hear them speak. No, that is not really correct—I could hear them *sing*.

It was if something had happened to my memory, and all that I had ever done to that point never really happened. All before was a dream. The only reality to me now was that face and those loving eyes. I was afraid to speak and retreated from the room to regain my composure. Yet, every time I closed my eyes, I could only remember hers and that soft smile and gentle voice. Where in my life would I ever find the courage to approach such a person and say anything of consequence? It was at that moment that I realized how alone I had been all of my life, and that, no matter what I had thought of myself in the past, I had never been a whole person.

I wanted to touch her, just to see if she were real. But I didn't know how. My touch would never be gentle enough for her fragile beauty. After days of trying, I found myself alone with her and knew at that moment that my life had changed; I had stopped loving myself more than I now loved another person. I didn't so much want to possess her as to be possessed by her. To be near her would be enough from that point on in my life. I now had found true meaning, true virtue, true adventure, and true love. For the first time, I wanted to surrender to something greater than myself: Love.

As I reflect back on it now, it is obvious that I grow more in love with her each day. Through her I have come to know the meaning of contentment. But, strangely, I find myself selfish again, just in a much different way. I am becoming jealous of any real time we are apart, because, unlike when I was young, I know I will not live forever. What gift of time we have left together will be as those years before—an instant, a flash, a moment.

Now I can finally rest and need to search no more. For in her I have found my enough. Anything more would be diminishment. I am finally a whole person. I am in love with love, and after this, what more could I ever want?

AN OPEN LETTER TO THE UNITED STATES MARINE CORPS

"Semper Fi"

Before even trying to respond to your very moving words, you have touched in me a chord of emotion and passion so long silent, but which now I must give voice. As you know, I always try to see where we stand in the moving light that is called our history. This light does not exist solely to illuminate the deeds of men or even nations, but rather it is able to reveal the truth of their actions and intentions. Time is the best test of truth!

Also, as you again well know, I am a man of words. Words have a life of their own. They not only have meaning but power as well. Every human institution and endeavor that attempts to stand this litmus test of time and truth has, as its sole foundation, words. America is not a place, an institution, a group of people and buildings; rather, it is an idea that exists only as long as men can and will dare to dream that liberty, freedom, justice, and equality are possible.

Men are imperfect, and all things that they try to build are therefore imperfect as well. Only twice in human history have men had the ability to even come near to a perfect idea and then try with all of the courage, desire, and will they could muster to establish that idea in reality. Both of these attempts are somewhat related.

The first is Christianity, an attempt to free the soul of every man from the slavery of evil, sin, and guilt. Even this—the greatest that can be thought or attempted by man—exists only as an idea, for if but one generation was to forget this FAITH or not put it into practice, it would pass from existence.

The other is the United States of America. This, for the first time, was a serious attempt to establish and bring into existence a society based on the ideas of "PURE VIRTUE." Men believed, for the first time, that freedom, liberty, justice, mercy, and equality would not be words only to be debated and defined in an academic context or restricted to philosophical or political debate; instead, these ideas would become real, present, and true.

As I said before, men are imperfect, and so this attempt at living these virtuous ideals was also an imperfect attempt. But therein lies its beauty. Only heaven is perfect, and by no means was America to be "Paradise on Earth." On the contrary, it was meant to be an expression and an atmosphere where men of courage, wisdom, and grace could try to live and put into practice what they believed. This very attempt at living virtue and truth was to be, by its very nature, a threat to every human establishment or society that did not have as its foundation stone the virtues of freedom and equality.

Therefore since our very beginning, from the birth of the idea that is our nation, we were and still are the enemy of all other powers and institutions that seek to exist on the backs of its citizens rather than in their minds, hearts, and souls.

Here then forced upon us by history and the nature of

men are two choices:

- First, deny what we say we believe and be destroyed. And let the possibility of a nation based on virtue pass from the hearts and minds of men.
- Second, have the courage to protect and defend what we say we believe and to fight for our very survival if necessary, realizing that this fight will last as long as there is evil in this world and in the hearts of men who hate virtue.

Now the questions of how best to fight, who should protect these virtues, and who should be trusted with the existence and perpetuation of this our great dream? We would need men as virtuous as the dream itself. We would need men willing, at a moment's notice, to rally to the call of liberty and freedom, with a commitment and fury unknown in human history. We would need men who could love without letting emotion rule their actions, fight with passion without a thought of personal cost or comfort. We would need men who understand that the true cost of freedom and liberty is their very lives. That to love America and what it stands for is to forever, in their lives, love all else a little less.

It is from this need to defend virtue, to defend this dream, that the idea of the United States Marine Corps was born. The MARINE CORPS is not the bully, strong-arm of American will in foreign policy. The MARINE CORPS does not exist to make a statement; it exists only to make a difference in the lives of people in this world who know and love freedom and liberty. This single fact of existence allows for no misunderstanding by our enemies as to our intent or purpose, and this is why we may never be loved by the rest of the world. But make no mistake, the UNITED STATES MARINE CORPS is and will always be RESPECTED by the rest of the world!

Contrary to what anyone else might think or say, a person does not JOIN the Marine Corps; rather, a person must BECOME a Marine! A person must be stripped of everything in their lives that they ever thought was important. A person must be stripped down to their very identity as a person and then be REBORN as a Marine. Many people will try and may even begin this process, but it is the MARINE CORPS alone that will decide if they are worthy of the uniform and title UNITED STATES MARINE.

To become a MARINE is to never again be a single person or stand alone. A MARINE is born into a new family unlike any that has ever existed or has ever been known or understood. A MARINE stands shoulder to shoulder in the corridors of history and looks from left to right and can see the long line of greatness that came before and will come after. A MARINE realizes that, no matter what he does that might seem as a great deed, it is only the greatness of the MARINE CORPS that truly matters. The Honor of the Corps is his honor. The Courage of the Corps Is hls courage. The Truth of the Corps is his truth. The MARINE CORPS values personal bravery but honors courage more. Courage is the ability to make your life's actions always consistent with what you say you believe.

A MARINE knows that if he must raise his fist to defend this great nation that he loves, there stands beside him brothers with hands open to help him in his fight. He will never stand alone. If he should be called to pay the greatest price that this nation can demand – his life – his brothers will carry his body from the field of valor. He will be forever remembered for his deeds of honor, not in books or on monuments of stone but in the heart of every person that loves freedom and honor and who dares to try to follow him in the CORPS!

To be a MARINE is to know and understand that every person in this nation owes their very freedom to his sacrifice and training and that he neither requires nor demands any public show of thanks. To wear the uniform of the UNITED STATES MARINE CORPS surpasses any emotion that would be generated by poor attempts at gratitude of non-Marines!! What matters most is that another MARINE looks into his eyes and says in silence, "Well done brother!"

Most people will never know any of these feelings or emotions, because they haven't got what it takes to serve our great nation as a member of the MARINE CORPS! So be proud, and if you are accused of being conceited, tell people that it is just detectable pride. Remember that it isn't bragging if you can really do it! Remember to stay motivated always and, if you need a little reminder or help, simply look up at our flag. If that doesn't re-motivate you, find another line of work, because the MARINE CORPS isn't for you!!

Sorry for the long epistle, but I don't know how to say what I feel about my Marine Corps in a few words; it has taken me the actions of a lifetime so far. I am very proud of you and have you in my prayers and thoughts always.

YOU WILL MAKE A GREAT MARINE!!

Love and Peace,
In Christ and the Corps,

O'Bryan USMC (Ret)

ON LEADERSHIP

Before there can be any discussion about ethical, moral, or any type of true leadership, past or present, there first must be a general agreement on the exact nature of leadership and the qualities and attributes of those with the responsibility and grace to exercise it.

Contrary to what most people in this country think, a leader is not someone with the power or desire and force to make people follow them. A leader is a person with the intelligence, judgment, courage, and humility to make people seek them out and want to follow them.

Leadership has no limits and bounds where it might be found. It is never defined or confined by such categories as age, sex, or position. Leadership has less to do with power and everything to do with service. The true measure of leadership is never its weight but its light. It has almost nothing to do with acquiring things; it has everything to do with distribution. Leadership never concerns itself with ownership but is always understood in the context of stewardship.

A leader is a person who can distinguish between the mathematics of justice and the arithmetic of envy. A leader has the ability to surround himself with people that make up for the areas of his inadequacies and then not fear them. His goal is not control but coordination.

The power that should be the sole focus of a true leader is the ultimate power; the greatest power found on earth and in the history of mankind. It is not the power to dominate or subject others to one person's will. The truest and greatest power is that which occurs when a person with vision meets people with dreams. This power can change not only the world but the very lives, spirits, and nature of all the people in this world.

It is an interesting paradox that a crisis does not make any person a leader any more than a battle makes a person a hero or a coward. The great crisis, like the fierce battle, serves only to reveal among us those who we recognize as leaders as well as those we call heroes and cowards.

True leaders should always put the good of all those people entrusted into their safe keeping first. They have the courage to risk their position as leaders because they will always exercise their judgment to do what they believe is right and not do that which is popular simply to maintain their position as the leader.

In today's world those people who are supposed to be our leaders always seem to sell themselves cheaply, for they strive to be liked by those they lead when they should work instead with all that is in them to be respected and loved. When a leader has the respect and love of the people, it shows that the leader has made the difference in the personal lives of those led and not just in the circumstances of the situations. These people are leaders not because of their opinions but because of their judgment and the fact that they will always take responsibility for the actions of themselves and their subordinates.

There is an old saying about leadership: "You can always delegate the authority but never the responsibility."

A leader always maintains an atmosphere of intellectual freedom and challenges the people they lead to think for themselves and not to think as the leader thinks. If you are ever in an intellectual situation where the success of your actions is based only on how the leader thinks, then it is not leadership at all but rather gross indoctrination!

A leader is not a person without fear; they are someone who has more courage than fear. They never try to define their worth and position by what they don't do, i.e., "Well, I don't kill," or "I don't steal." The actions of leadership define who and what they are. Again, a leader is never a person who tells you what they stand for. A leader is someone who by his very nature and courage and by his consistent actions makes clear what he will or will not stand for.

Leaders do not worry about what history will say of them and their actions and decisions. They do not worry about the hole that will be left when they are gone. Rather, they work to be remembered for the light that they gave while they were here.

A true leader knows when to advance and when to step down. He recognizes the basic difference between being in charge and taking the responsibility, and then takes action to stay level-headed in whatever situation in which they find themselves.

You might think that it is impossible to be this kind of a leader because he or she would have to be a saint. Remember: a saint is just a sinner who keeps trying. You don't have to be perfect to be a leader. You must, however, be able to distinguish between perfection for yourself and those for which you have responsibly and excellence.

A leader remembers always that grace builds upon nature.

FINDING MY HOME

In the life of every child, sooner or later comes the desire to run away from home. Sometimes it's just a threat against their parents or guardians in response to unwelcome discipline or something negative in the child's life at that point in time. What the child never realizes, though, is that it is really impossible to run away from home. That's because home isn't a place or an object, it is a state of mind and being.

Over the course of a child's maturing process, in tiny degrees, he or she begins to drift away from the love that binds us to a place or structure. Soon these bonds are so strained that they break, usually in subtle silence and not in an observable explosion. Over time they become aware that something is missing from the fabric of their spirit and soul.

People then spend the rest of their lives in a never-ending quest to reestablish that which they find to be missing. In their quest they may come close or even have that which is most similar to the time and place that they are looking for, but never again will they find that *home* they left long ago in this material world. They must then ask themselves, "Where is this remembered place of family and love to be found?"

What they must realize is that finding the home that they think they have lost is really only a matter of perspective. They will never find this treasured memory outside of themselves. Their search then must take place within themselves, and that is where they will find that true home and loving place that they left long ago.

The greatest revelation in this quest is to find that, if they search in their hearts, their soul, and their spirit in truth, each and every place in their memory where they have ever loved and where they have ever been loved in return is that place they seek called "home."

HEALING

"He touched me and made me whole" — Southern Gospel Song

If you are ill and go to see a professional in the medical community and are cured, then the person with whom you had contact is a scientist. If, on the other hand, you see a person in the medical community and you are healed, you are a physician. In order to exercise the power of healing, a person must surrender to a higher authority, a higher good, a higher power. The person must have faith and trust and become a willing instrument in the hands of God, the divine physician.

Healing isn't so much a matter of the patient getting better as it is a matter of the ill person again moving forward in his or her life. When a person is very sick, they seem to lose sight of the future and see only the high points of the past as their glory. When a person is healed, they can once more see the promise that the future holds. They can once again focus on tomorrow, and they have been restored to a faith and hope in tomorrow.

To heal is to kill fear, to reignite a love of life that seemed to have vanished. The person again has energy, a will, and a purpose in their life. Renewed in them is a promise of a valued time to come, no matter how short that future is. When a person is healed, all that is to come is simplicity itself. They can see with uncomplicated eyes the road to be followed, and they can rejoice in the commonest of pleasures. Each step that they take from the point beyond the moment of healing becomes sacred. Everything that touches them again for the first time becomes holy, and every word that they speak and hear becomes important.

To be healed does not mean that you are no longer ill; it means that you have accepted your illness and can see its value in your life to unite you with the suffering and death of Christ. Your healing is a grace that allows you to carry your cross step-by-step with the wounded Jesus and offer to God with His Son the words, "If this cup will not pass, then your will be done." It is the grace to embrace your suffering as something positive. It is the grace to understand and realize that the pain can be offered back to the Father as a gift and to demonstrate the depth of your love for His will and His plan.

All healing comes from God and is therefore good by its very nature. Evil does not have the power to heal. Evil has the power to deceive a person into believing that they are cured, and when the truth of their condition is known to them, they lose all faith and hope which is always the goal of evil. Instead of rejoicing in the grace of God, they despair in what they are deceived into believing is His lack of caring, His lack of love for the person. They never see their illness as means to bring them closer to God; they see their pain as a sign of His abandonment, and they feel that they are truly alone. They reject the very Grace that they need to draw closer to God, and that is the Grace of humility. When a person is truly humble and pride is no longer in the center, they realize that they can never bear the pain alone, and that

73

when it is offered back to the Father it soon becomes a sweet gift, a source of love and a testament to their faith. In their healing, their body may still suffer, but their spirit and soul may grow beyond measure. They realize that, even if today they cannot walk, in a short time they will fly!

Since the earliest days of the Christian church, power and healing have always been accomplished by the "laying on of hands." The person who has become the instrument of God allows His grace and power to flow through themselves. Today a physician performs this in the same manner. It is through His faith and trust in God that you are healed, and not through his education.

EVERY MAN A KING

The late Sen. Huey Long of Louisiana used to have a saying: "Every man a king." I don't believe that every man is born a king, but I do believe every man can choose to become a king.

True nobility is not found in a crown on a head or in silk robes on the body. You are not royal because you sit on a purple cushion upon a golden throne. You are not noble because of what you have; you are king because of what you are. True nobility is found in the depth of your heart and the power of your mind.

If you are a lover of life and all that it brings, both good and bad; if honor knows your name; if the poor and weak call you friend and brother; if freedom, liberty, and justice aren't just words but your code of life; if you can reach high and fall many times but rise higher with each new try; if you can take time to listen when you really want to speak; if you try always to extend an open hand and use only a clenched fist to protect those who cannot protect themselves; if you know there is always someone and something greater than yourself; if you can look at the stars at night and say with all your heart, "Why not?"; if you can feel the chains of another person's oppression and struggle with all of your might to break these links of injustice and set them free; if you value wisdom and learning as great tools and not as weapons; if you are willing to give your life for those that you love to make a difference in their world, not just a statement; if you learn to rule yourself with strict discipline and yet have a gentle, understanding nature of the weaknesses of others; if you can reign in your passions governing their actions and temper your faults; if you can truly forgive yourself and others, and forever use virtue as your guide and beacon in life; if you can be given power and realize the burden of service to others that pure power demands; if these are all truths within you, then you are already truly a king among your fellow man.

THE POWER TO TRANSFORM

Human beings have not the power, gifts, or ability to create anything. Creation is the most unique power in the universe and is reserved to God alone. It is His power to bring anything into being simply by willing it to be! He thinks of it and it exists.

Mankind, on the other hand, can only manipulate that which is already here. They can alter it but can create nothing, really. Children, however, have a unique gift and talent of their own. They have the power to transform almost anything that they see and know. They do this by the powers that are their loves, intellect, courage, insight, heart, spirit, and soul. They can take almost any artifact or idea in history and alter its meaning. They can reveal the hidden truth and deepest meanings found in the simplicity of the object or thought. They can only change the meaning, but its fundamental nature and purpose stays the same.

If you don't believe this, simply look at the Cross. Look how people and time have changed it from what it was once used for, and now they have changed its meaning to what it now stands for!

SUNSET TO SON-RISE

At many different times and places during my life I have found myself pondering about what happens when we have seen the last of this world. I know all of the answers and reasons that religion offers, and yet there is always—even in faith—the mystery of it all. I have found that, when asked, most people say they want to go to heaven but just don't want to die to get there. This is man's basic fear of the dark, the unknown.

Now, after much thought, prayer, and life, there is within me a very different belief about that moment we call *death*. For I no longer believe it is a moment like switching a light on and off. Now it is light; now it is dark! No matter how it might look in earthly time, I believe each of us dies at the same rate or speed, if you wish. It seems to me that there is no such thing as an instant death.

As for me now, I believe death is a process like everything else in life and not simply an event. This process is like sitting alone on a quiet deserted beach, watching the beautiful sunset. The sun goes down slowly, and our whole world is changed; the colors become endless and subtle. As the sun goes below the horizon, its light fades and the warmth is gone; soon it is just a memory. Then, with a sudden realization, we begin to discern the tiny seeds of light that appear in the black velvet sky one at a time, until the heavens are once again ablaze with these stars. There is no end to their number and no limit to their glory.

When we see these stars, we are not afraid or bewildered. We are at peace and our soul, our spirit is calm. In our heart we know that the sun that has just faded and left us alone; that it will return in the morning and it will once more be light.

So, I believe, it is with our death. We sit and wait unafraid because we have hope and trust given to us by the tiny lights in the darkness. We can have such faith and hope because we have seen so many sunsets and sunrises. We can sit quietly in the dark and be unafraid because we have the promise of the Father that He will send us His light. Now the difference is that for the first and only time in our existence we wait for that light that is God. We realize with great excitement that we are waiting for the *Son*-rise.

I believe that death does not occur because the soul has reached a point where it can't return to this existence. I believe that death is the point where the soul that is basking in the Glorious Light of God no longer wishes or desires to return to this existence.

THE MANY FACES OF CHRISTMAS

"And the Word was made Flesh"

Christmas has many names and many faces. The voices and sounds are as varied as the ways in which it is celebrated. It is not a celebration that is exclusive to any one person or culture. Colors tell us when the time of this holy celebration is about to begin. The universal excitement of the people of all ages is unmatched at any other time in our yearly calendar.

Yet, when you begin to sit back and, as a quiet observer, try not to get caught up in the material aspects of all that is going on around you, you become aware of the much broader scope and depth of these blessed hours. The many physical symbols that have been attached to this beautiful time might confuse you into believing that they can somehow define in your sight what is going on in your heart. I can assure you that they cannot.

The power and magnitude of this event in the history of mankind, when the finite touched the infinite, is beyond words, sounds, pictures, or symbols.

Christmas is not just a tree, beautifully wrapped gifts, sacred hymns, or big elves dressed in red and white pulled through the air by flying deer. These are there to help us understand and motivate us to reach the level of joy we should be feeling and spreading. But even these are not Christmas.

This feast is not simply an earthly celebration. It is one of the few times where the feelings of Heaven and those of Earth are the same. Men and angels rejoice, for God, our loving Father, has truly fulfilled His promise made to Adam in the garden of Paradise.

For me, the most beautiful symbol of this magnificent celebration actually takes place in the dark stillness of the Holy Night. I love the idea that in one instant I am in the darkest night, quiet, cold, and frightened, yet still feel peaceful. Then, in the next, I am bathed in the most exquisite light that a human being could hope to see, feel, know, and imagine.

It is to comprehend and finally understand in one moment of existence the awesome power of God our Father and the true depth of His love for us. It is to know that, no matter what else may happen in my life, I will never be in the dark again.

Seeing this example of Christ in all of His helpless humanity, I can finally begin to know and become aware of my poorest self. It is in this recognition of my absolute humble human condition that I may finally discover, with the help of His Grace, and begin to understand what the words, "To adore God, with my whole heart, soul and spirit" really means.

There is one other symbol that has great meaning in my heart at this time. It is to see that helpless child on his bed of straw after being born in a stable. Yet, both shepherds and kings kneel and adore this child side by side. In Loving Him, He has made all men equal for the first time in history. As the angels sing to announce His birth, all who come to behold Him see that He is The Pure Truth Incarnate. He is that ancient promise fulfilled. He is the One True King. He is the One True Master Shepherd. He is the best that man can be and the Power and Majesty that is God.

I am humbled to believe that he gifted me with His presence. He wants me as His own, He cares about me, and He Loves me. He calls me by name and tells me I am His child. Through His gift of Grace and this Faith, I can now also begin to understand the meaning of the word Humility.

OF WHAT IS LOVE?

"And now these three remain: faith, hope, and love. But the greatest of these is love."
— 1 Corinthians 13

This is a question that people in love never seem to ask. They don't need to know. To people in love, the word defines itself not in letters or syllables but in feelings and actions. This lifts it above all other human experiences. It is totally unique to any other feeling a human being can have, and it has its own unique memory. It can never be forgotten. To remember love is to love once more. Love never ends!

The power that is love never pulls or pushes; it neither leads nor follows; it guides. It has no limits, boundaries or conditions where it cannot exist and grow. It can only really increase by being shared and given, and there is no diminishment. The capacity of a person to love is only contingent upon their capacity to be loved. It can be quiet or loud but can never be silent to the heart and soul. It is in constant motion and never rests. It can't be qualified or quantified.

Love has both the ability to blind and make clear. It can

motivate but never restrict. It can be seen but not touched. Love is its own nourishment. It is the strongest force in creation and can never be destroyed. It has no arithmetic or science. No textbook or formula. It has the property of color but one that cannot be seen but rather is felt. It is always warm and never cold. It is never hungry or tired. Love never compromises but always yields. It desires the lesser part always but is itself always the greatest. It never stands alone but seeks company. It heals but never punishes or offends. Love is its own music and verse, its own song, its own art. It lifts but never crushes or oppresses. It is true freedom to the slave and true justice for those who have been falsely accused. It can never bare false witness. It is the greater part of mercy and the true foundation of hope.

Love is from God, and it is God. When we love it is then that we are most like our Father and His Son. If love never ends, and we can and do love, then by this grace and gift is our everlasting promise of life if we become love.

A FEW QUESTIONS FOR MY FELLOW CHRISTIANS

1. When did we as Christians start hating the SIN and the SINNER as well?
2. When did we stop being Christians and become Jewish because of the force in our lives we give to the Old Testament?
3. When did the hundreds of laws of HATE in the Old Testament become greater than the 2 Great Laws of LOVE from Jesus in the New Testament?
4. When did Christians go from a people who were identified by their LOVE and SERVICE to each other and to their community and become a people concerned with POWER, EXCLUSION, and ELITISM?
5. When did Christians become so afraid of the world and being in the world that they lost their FAITH in the PROTECTIVE POWER of God and His Spirit AND in the power found in the NAME OF JESUS CHRIST TO OVERCOME any power found in EVIL?
6. When did Christians start believing that Satan was more powerful and knowledgeable than God?

7. When did Christians start preaching to themselves in their comfortable churches and forget the Face of Christ is found in those poor souls no longer welcome or found in those churches?

8. When did Christians forget the difference between a Disciple and an Apostle?

9. When did Christians so rejoice in being the sheep that didn't go astray that they no longer help the Good Shepherd seek those that did?

10. When did Christians go from feeding all of Christ's sheep to only feeding Christ's sheep that we like or can relate to?

11. When did Christians forget that "The last shall be first, and the first shall be last"? Our place is LAST!

12. When did we as Christians, either by our actions or silence, come to support other so-called Christians in their campaign of HATE, BIGOTRY, IGNORANCE, and RACISM, and help them TO HEAP MORE PAIN on the PEOPLE OF GOD suffering the greatest loss that they can know, that of the loss of a child? When did we decide to help this sick, misguided cult of HATE to pervert the message of Christ, "Blessed are those who mourn, for they shall be comforted," in order to inflict as much pain as is possible and deprive the sufferers of the HOPE, FELLOWSHIP, and fraternal LOVE that is the second of the Great Commandments of your Redeemer?

13. When did we as Christians decide in our communities that Salvation must come in under budget and ask its members for money more times than asking them for LOVE?

14. When did we as Christians become much more concerned about where we pray than how and what

we pray?

15. When did we as Christians forget that Christ's Kingdom is not of this world?

16. When did we decide that only SOME lives are SACRED and not ALL LIFE?

17. When did we stop recognizing Christ's face in those people we find difficult to look at?

18. When are Christians going to learn that there is a great deal of difference between QUESTIONING something and DOUBTING it? Didn't Saint Paul tell us to "Question everything," and Albert Einstein tell us to "Have faith"?

SOME THINGS I HAVE OBSERVED, LEARNED, OR FELT IN MY LIFE

In my life I have discovered and learned many mysterious, wonderful and beautiful things. I have been to great heights and very low depths, both emotionally and physically. Some of this knowledge came about by accident, some by reading, some by poor judgment, some through observation, and some simply by listening. I wouldn't change a thing in my past, good or bad, because I am the person I am today because of the good and not so good things that have touched me. I like who I am, what I am, and where I am at this point in my life. To change anything in my past would alter my present, and to me this would be unsatisfactory.

These things I know:

- The most important thing I know in my life is that, no matter what other people may say, love is forever. Love can't be killed or forgotten no matter how hard I try. It is the only experience that is always present to me without regard to time and space. I may have broken my arm when I was young, and it may have been very painful at the time, but when the accident is remembered I feel no pain. This is not true with love. For to remember love is to love once more. I may think that I now hate what once was loved, but then I realize that hate is not the opposite of love – apathy – and that I still care.

- When I see a sunrise or a sunset, it doesn't matter how many people are around: I am alone. It is as if I am present in two worlds at the same time. While watching the beauty before me, it is one of the few times that I am not thinking of anything else; I am just in a state of being, connected mystically with what I see. I pose no questions to myself of how or why. I find that I don't want an explanation or definition because any answer would be diminishment. It is as if God gave that glorious sight to me personally to enjoy. It is my personal gift from Him.

  I also realize how small I really am and how much I am in need of God's protection. Without His hand, I would be forever lost and destroyed.

- Heaven was not created for the perfect souls but for the imperfect ones. I must never seek perfection; rather, I should strive to become excellent. This means that I will always be dependent on God's grace and not on my own devices; that I should strive to love imperfection because, in so doing, I can love myself and the humanity around me. I can only love to my capacity to be loved.

- A person's character is never built or defined by telling

people what they stand for. The depth and foundation of your character can only be defined and grow by having the courage to show the world what you refuse to stand for.

- I should never strive to make a statement with my life; I should strive always and in every way to make a difference with my life.

- When I pass from this life, I should strive to be remembered not for the hole that is left when I cease to exist but rather for the light that I gave when I was present.

- I should never seek to find in an explosion that which can be found in a whisper.

- One person can make a difference.

- I can never really own anything. All material things that are entrusted to me while I live must be protected, not abused or exploited, and all must be improved. I incur a debt of use for all things that I touch in this life, and my goal must always be to leave this material world better than I found it. There is no such thing as ownership; there is only stewardship.

- Quantitative data will never lead me to a qualitative conclusion. How many can never tell me how good or how bad.

- Life is a journey and not a destination. It is a process,

and it doesn't happen in a vacuum.

- When your dog dies, you never really get over it because he gave you the only unconditional love you will ever know in this world.

- When I sit and watch a steam run its silvery course, it is also carrying my soul and spirit with it. It has kidnapped my imagination and lets me dream about what I can do, what I can become, and how far I can go. The form of my life is closely related to the rivers and streams. Life flows, sometimes quickly, sometimes slowly, but it moves on at a pace that cannot be altered by human beings. We ride it swiftly, slowly. There are rocks and rapids and, yes, even still waters, but we are always moving, flowing, changing. It is a constant that we have no power to fight, and yet we must never surrender, remembering that the water is constantly moving, changing. This movement always indicates life. To stop is to die.

- No matter how many times I look up at the stars in the night sky on a clear summer's evening I will always discover one more star that I never saw before.

- Greatness is not always found in the person doing great deeds; rather, greatness is more often found in the person who is able to distinguish in their life those deeds which are great. Greatness is giving voice to those who can't speak for themselves. It's giving your power to the helpless, reaching out with an open hand and heart to raise the lowly, not out of pity or shame, but because you have learned to love humanity. Greatness always reaches to give protection and power to the weak, looking for the good in all people first, and giving them the respect and dignity that they merit simply by being people. Any person who tries to live their life in the service of others becomes the greatest of all. Service and commitment to others lifts a person to both a spiritual and moral nobility.

- In any difficult situation, rather than asking what is going on, your first question should be "What can I do to help"?

- Most people do not know when and how they will die, but they will always have the choice of whom and what they will be when they do. Death doesn't end life, just our simple ability to animate our bodies.

- The interesting thing about fame, fortune, and status is that if you have no character before you possess these things you will never have character after you possess these things.

- The wealthy should be pitied because they can no longer have the dream that money, social position, or power can buy happiness; they already know these things cannot.

- There is a great difference between being childish and childlike.

- The more we know that we are being looked to as an

example, the better example we should become.

- In your life you must learn to communicate in two different languages: first, a language of words; second, a language of deeds that are consistent with the first.

- All people must be taught and must understand both intellectually and internally that victory and winning are not the same thing, just as defeat and losing are not the same thing.

- When you wait to act because you are worried about what others may think of your actions, you live a weak and compromised life.

- Power is the drug of history.

- Courage is not a single action but rather a habit that takes a lifetime to acquire.

- You can never help others by extending a closed hand.

- If you want to begin to know yourself, when you get into a car, don't turn on the radio as the first action after you start the engine. Do not treat the silence that you find as an enemy. Silence is not a blanket; it is a window to your heart, soul, and spirit.

- There is a tremendous difference between questioning something and doubting it.

- In every life there are both problems and mysteries. To

be happy, try to solve the problems and then try to live with the mystery, and then learn to distinguish between the two.

- Most people don't know the difference between a fact and a truth.

- Our dreams must not be thought of as the limit to which we may aspire; rather, our dreams should be the goals we know we can reach in faith and hope.

- A person's destiny is truly met when their heart unites itself with all that is good in the world, all that is painful in the world, and all that is worthwhile in the world. All that which is called the human condition has value when it is shared, carried, and embraced with love by one person in the name of all people. Open your hand to others in need. Open your mind to others seeking understanding not judgment. Open your heart to all in most need of love starting with yourself.

- It isn't always the first pound of love given that is the most important and the most helpful; sometimes the last ounce that is offered counts the most and has the greatest effect.

- To truly hear and understand what is going on in the world that surrounds you, you must listen not only with your ears but with all of your senses. Silence is not an absence of noise; it is a condition of spirit where you become one with all that is around you. Nature can speak to your pure, simple, and humble self. Let what you hear become what you know. Let it change you and help you to become not what you want to become but also what you need to become.

- Sometimes I need to sit and think and pray; other times I just need to sit.

- When I find something in another person that I dislike, I usually find that I dislike that same thing in myself.

- Very little of what I see, hear, or do is ever really complete.

- For me, education is as much a revelation of what I still don't know as it is what I do know.

- The greatest tool man has used to build his civilization and his greatest weapon to destroy his civilization is the same thing: WORDS. Words are all that we have. Every government, religion, nation, and belief is made of words. All of the institutions of men are simply ideas expressed as words. A man's word is his most powerful and valuable possession. To bring the validity and creditability of your word into doubt is to destroy the very essence of your most intimate identity.

- No matter what happens to us, our happiness is always a choice that we make. Refuse to be overcome by that which is bad, painful, or evil and you will find a hidden reserve of grace to rejoice in our human condition. Remember, to feel sadness, joy, love, pain, or despair means that we are still alive with the knowledge that all conditions in this life are temporary. No human condition, no matter how overwhelming, is ever constant. We are always in a state of transition. If we choose to become better, we will become better. If we chose to be defeated, we fail. In the end, we determine our emotional fate; to despair is to be overcome by the power to change. All that we must do is remember that we have a greater and stronger link to hope, faith, joy, and love than the negative situations in our human condition. We must always remember that if we loved and that we were loved is the first step to loving again. We must fight the dark times in our lives with the memories of the times, places, and people that brought us light. With the power of this remembered light, the weakness of darkness is vanquished once again by our faith in ourselves to once again believe in the power of a loving, hopeful heart.

- No matter how good your intention or how hard you try, you can never dream for another person.

- Bravery is but a momentary action whereas courage takes a lifetime to be recognized. Courage is not a single action but rather a condition of heart, soul, intellect, and will that takes an entire lifetime to develop and possess. This world will always have brave men and women. This world will always NEED and always DEMAND that there be courageous people to survive.

- If one person is punished unjustly and no one raises a

voice in protest then justice dies and mercy is still born.

- If one person is unjustly in chains and no one raises a voice in protest then we are all made slaves by that injustice.

- Law is the servant of men; men are not servants of the law. The individual must always come first.

- The greatest virtue is HONOR, followed very closely by LOVE, LOYALTY, and DUTY.

- People would get better results if they would first try to raise another's spirit than to crush another's dignity.

- A leader is not someone with the power to MAKE others follow them; rather, a leader possesses the gifts and talents to make others WANT to follow him. Leadership is never about power, but it is everything about service.

- People who are chosen to lead are invested with that position by others because of a great faith in their judgment to make the right choices for the good of the whole. To paraphrase Edmund Burke: When a leader sacrifices his judgment to the opinions of the people that elected them, he ceases to be a leader.

- Politicians are almost never leaders. Their first action after getting elected is to try to get elected again. They always seem to sacrifice their judgment to the opinion of people who elected them. This action betrays that trust.

- There is a great difference between a gift and a present. A present is given to you to do with as you please – you own it, it is yours. A gift, on the other hand, is bestowed upon you, without your ownership, to be used in the noblest of all callings: service to others! A gift belongs only to God! He shares it with a few favored souls to be used as an instrument to bring about His plan and kingdom here among his believers. You don't have to believe to be given one of His gifts; you just have to be accepting.

- For me, music is really liquid scripture.

- In life it doesn't really matter where a person comes from; all that really matters is the direction a person is heading.

- Wizards really do exist in this world. But wizards aren't people with the ability to perform magic; rather, they are people with the heart and power to bring the magic out of you. Always seek out your wizard in this world, and once you find them, never let them go.

- Finding your dream is a beginning and not an end.

- More is communicated by a kiss and a gentle touch than all of the great words ever written.

- People who cannot see are not blind, and people who

cannot hear are not deaf; they are only handicapped. The blind and deaf are those who choose not to see or hear.

- Most people who run roadside produce stands can't spell cantaloupes correctly.

- Old age has very little to do with the number of years that a person has lived, but it has everything to do with attitude. I have met many young people who are old and many elderly people who are young. You become old the moment that you stop looking forward and can no longer face the future with hope and excitement. It is that instant when the past becomes your only real comfort.

- When people think of the past there are only three ways they can see it: 1) it was better than it was in reality, "The Good Old Days"; 2) it was worse than it was in reality, i.e., "I walked to school eight miles in snow up to my hips, uphill in both directions"; and 3) those blessed few who remember it as it really was.

- A blessing means simply to set something apart and remember that it is a gift from God. We should always strive to be a blessing to each other.

- The older you get, the easier it is to cry. It's the simple things we have and remember that make us cry the most.

- This would be a much better world if you didn't need a

signature or a lawyer to have a contract, but rather just a handshake or a simple "yes" in order to seal an agreement.

- My life would be much simpler if I could believe there really was a Santa Claus.

- It is much better to remember my blessings than to count my money.

- It is beyond my puny intellectual capacity to figure out why some words are contractions. When I write the word "don't," it is just as easy for me to write an "o" as it is to put in an apostrophe.

- Most people can't give you the definition of the word simple and not use a thousand words. When something is said to be simple it is no more and it is no less; it just is.

- All an atheist ever wants to talk about is God.

- When two people dwell in the land of love, it asks for no definitions, only demonstrations.

- It is very easy to accept the good, joyous, happy times in our human experience and see the positive changes they make in our nature, heart, soul, and disposition. The real trick is to accept the things that make us sad, knock us down, and seem unjust; to accept it when we are treated with a lack of mercy and get less than we think we deserve, less than what we believe is our fair share, and not let these things make us cynical. Instead, we must always strive for the ability to accept the God's grace in these situations to make us *better* not *bitter*. If we can't do this then weakness and evil wins!

- The so called "American Dream" is not a license to become rich and powerful. It has little to do with the acquisition of material possessions. The "American Dream" is exactly what it says it is: the freedom to believe that any dream in America can be yours. No person, institution, or establishment can take away a person's liberty and freedom to try and become better than they are. The "American Dream" is to know that you can really become anything you choose to be.

- If I love where I am, and I am loved where I am, I am home. (You have to read this one slowly.)

- If you want to stay young, always retain your passion for everything you do.

- The validity of a truth is never dependent on how many people believe something or how deeply they believe something. One person can be right. The only great tragedy is when you lack the courage to speak that truth to the crowd.

- Geniuses are good to have around for the plans; however, it's the hard worker who gets most things done.

- You can accomplish almost anything when you work with others, as long as you don't care who gets the credit.

- I would rather have a rainy Monday than a rainy Friday.

- Every person must never lose their desire and ability to play.

- I am quicker to pardon wrong actions done by myself than I am to pardon them in others.

- To be a really successful worker and get things done, we must be able to distinguish between when it is time to REST and when it is time to QUIT.

- The older I get, each time I say "good bye" to someone I love, the more I fear that it might be true.

- As my life has changed, so has my soul and spirit. I find that I am becoming simpler; that I require fewer definitions; that intellect is less a weapon and more of a tool; that I have a greater need to share what I truly believe about this world and all of the good things in it; that I am finally becoming humbled by my gifts and talents; that I'm not as complex as I thought I was.

- True strength is not found in power but in humility and the capacity to love.

- People really desire limits, boundaries, and walls.

Those that scream loudest for anarchy and chaos are simply calling for order by using its most extreme voice.

- The forces of nature and human nature may determine what we become in our lives, but it is LOVE alone or the lack of LOVE that determines who we truly become.

- A grave is sad for two reasons: first, because it shows the end of a life; second, because it shows the end of a dream.

- Most of the time, when someone you love tries to push you away, they are really trying to pull you near.

- It is a very strange fact that the most ignorant people I have met in my life are also the most educated.

- The older most people grow the more they seem to fear the truth.

- Almost every negative quality in a human being is learned, such as hate and bigotry. This fact alone is enough to give me hope for the future. Someday maybe these lessons won't be taught to our children.

- If you want to know what the future could be, don't go to a so-called fortune teller or a mystic, just take 15 minutes and listen to the dreams of a group of children.

- When a person's heart stops beating isn't the only sign of their death; they also die when they lose the virtues of hope and faith in their life.

- If you want to know how deeply two people are in love with each other, count the number of times that they use plural pronouns in a 30-minute conversation about their relationship.

- I am still very happy that while watching a parade, no matter what the occasion, I still get a lump in my throat when I hear patriotic music and see my country's flag go by.

- No matter how many times I visit Washington D.C. and see all of the great building and sights, I am still most moved at the Vietnam Memorial. I still cry each time I see the gifts that others have left behind as part of the story of their lives, and how they are trying to touch so gently one more time the lives of those who we finally recognize as true heroes. At long last we can say in our hearts, "Welcome home, dear brothers and sisters. Your sacrifice was not wasted or in vain. You have finally found your final resting place, not only in our hallowed ground but in our deepest love as well."

- Friendship is a form of adoption. In life, next to love, the greatest gift that you can give to another person and to yourself is friendship.

- Power in its purest form is not that which overcomes or conquers but rather that which frees and elevates all that it touches.

- Nature reveals; man conceals. Most people can't seem to believe that the greatest truth uses the fewest words, and that love really needs no words at all.

- People of weak intellect and spirit use confusion as a weapon.

- The greatest criminals are not those people who rob, steal, injure, or kill others; rather, they are those who keep others in ignorance of truth and fear of change, so as to exercise their own petty will and weak sense of purpose and order on those they deem to be beneath them.

- Every day is a gift to be opened slowly, and every stranger is a potential friend waiting for an invitation to be welcomed and loved.

- No matter how hard people try they can never insult a truly humble man.

- Human beings are the only creatures on this planet that can be blinded by what they see.

- Conflict does not make men heroes or cowards; it simply reveals which men are heroes and which men are cowards.

- Faith is a much higher grace and power than knowledge. In order to have true faith, you must admit to the possibility that everything you believe to be true or correct may indeed be false. Yet with true faith you can choose to keep on believing in spite of those doubts. This is what gives faith its great singular value and worth.

- Any civilization or society that chooses to freely kill its children, no matter what the reason, kills its own future and condemns itself to destruction. With the death of these children, the society denies itself the energy it needs to grow. It kills the potential it needs to change. This is why abortion is not only a sin it is also a crime against the future.

- A Christian can only understand the true meaning of Christ's suffering a death upon the Cross when it is understood in the context, faith, and power of the empty tomb.

- Dreams may be the only experience in the human condition that have neither limits or boundaries.

- In the world today there are too many people that are trying to be envied for what material goods they possess when they should strive to be admired for whom and what they are.

- The greatness and the security of America are not defined by our strongest and wealthiest citizens. Our greatness is defined and found in our weakest citizens. Here, the poorest and least able to contribute are given equal protection and value under our

Constitution. They are made whole and have an equal share in this great "American Dream."

- No matter how hard I try not to be, I am a hopeless romantic. I am in love with love. I believe that every story can have a happy ending; that the good guy gets the girl at the finish. I believe that justice and truth will prevail and that good will always defeat evil, no matter how long it takes. I truly believe to stay alive is to stay in love.

- One of the hardest things that we will all have do at some point in our lives is kiss a dream goodbye.

- One of the truly great tragedies in life is when a person doesn't know the difference between their loves and their passions. Passions deal exclusively with any of their human activities, whereas human loves are exclusively limited to relationships with other human beings or oneself.

- Love is never a possession; it is a mission, a journey, a quest that will lead us to the only treasure we will take from this world when it is our time to leave.

- Believing in Heaven is like walking in a deep dark forest: You do not have to leave the trees to prove that the sky is there; you only have to look with faith to see that the sky is above the trees.

- True heroes may be defeated, but they will never be

vanquished.

- Selfish people can never love deeply or for very long. They lack the ability to share the one element that is essential to any loving relationships: themselves!

SOME SMALL BITES OF FOOD FOR THOUGHT

When the last person of a generation dies, and that person was a witness to great events, that human's experience goes from MEMORY to HISTORY!

All human life in all and any form is Sacred. Capital punishment then is just legally sanctioned human sacrifice upon the supposed high altar of justice, while keeping a blind eye toward the higher altar of mercy and the highest altar of mortality!

Riding a motorcycle is a great, but nobody messes with the man who drives an elephant!

If the world seems a dark place to you, don't blame it on evil. Maybe it is because people refuse to share or combine their light.

In the sound or in the silence
In the light or in the dark
In the height or in the depth
In the mind or in the heart
Where I have sought God I have found him!

I have found that most people who have no regard for life also feel no responsibility for the future!

"When you do it to the least, you do it also to me." – Christ

The two times in a person's life when they are the most least is just before they die and when they are not yet born.

One thing that has always puzzled me is why there would ever be silent letters in a written or spoken language. But then again, who is dumber: the one who started doing it or the people who keep doing it?
In scripture I have given up trying to find the key to those things I don't understand and am now making a greater effort to live those I do!

There is a vast difference between trying to relieve a person's suffering and ending their life!
I have found that it is impossible to insult a truly humble man!

When people tell me that they can't understand all of the evil that they see in the world, I tell them to rejoice, because that means that God has let them also see all of the Good in the world to make the comparison.

May people live their lives in fear of something. As a Christian I may not want to get shot, but I do not live in fear of being shot to death.

Where do I go today to find that long-lost nobility in America of service to others weaker than ourselves that made us the greatest nation on earth?

A love has to be unconditional, or it isn't love at all!

One of the most painful times in the life of any human being is when they realize that their parents have now become their children. But unlike the time after birth, when they began to grow stronger and more independent, in the case of their parents in old age, they only grow weaker and more dependent. Yet each burden is bearable if it is done in and with pure love.

A dream is a very fragile thing. It is made up of three parts: the mystical, the magical, and the material. I have had so many dreams in the night that only vanished with the dawn. I should be discouraged, but I am not because enough have come true to always keep me dreaming of what is really possible.

Seek not only to understand the parts of your life but to also understand the sum of your life experiences.

In life you will find that you really can't intimidate a genuine smart ass!

I have found that the things in my life that have kept me young are also those things that have given me the most light in my life: passion, love, friends, and my true vocation.

I have found in life that a person's character and spirit are only as deep as their loves in life.

True bravery does not come from an absence of fear but rather from the virtue of courage to overcome that fear. Doing what you love and loving what you do is not the same thing.

To me the saddest life of all is that which reaches death before dying.

Prayer can never be simply a conversation with God without also being a movement toward the object of that conversation.

Human beings always seem to underestimate all that can be accomplished with God's grace.

When you finally hear your dream calling, do not hesitate but answer immediately.

Life to me is not so much of a gift as it is a grace, a journey, and a test. Only at the end of a life lived with the constancy of grace can it expect the gift that has been promised.

No one can get to our suffering Lord without first climbing their own Calvary with Him.

No one can get to our Risen Lord without first knowing their empty tomb through Him.

No one can get to our heavenly Lord without first learning to let their spirit soar freely, as taught by a trusting grace given by Him.

Be careful when someone asks for your advice. They may not care as much about what you are saying as they do about wanting someone to blame things on when they screw things up!

HONOR-THE HIGHEST FOUNDATION OF ALL VIRTUES
(*GIVEN AT AN JROTC BANQUET IN BEAVER, PA., JUNE 2009*)

We use words to communicate what we want to express and have others understand. But in our language words not only have meaning, they also have power.

Some words can motivate, challenge, inspire, and move men hearts, spirits, and souls to do great deeds. But to really understand these special words, we don't so much need to have them in our mind but rather permanently carved in our heart, in our spirit, and on the very essence of our identity and being.

Some of these words can't be simply defined by other material words, for material words lack the power and ability to do this.

There are very special words called virtues. In order to truly understand virtuous words they must be demonstrated; they must be accompanied by actions. You can look in any dictionary and find the word honor, but simply knowing the meaning of this word won't make you honorable. To know what this word means, we must be around honorable people, see honorable actions, and know the honor of will. These people demonstrate honor to us. When we see the consistency of their words and actions, only then do we understand honor! And when they pass it on to others, it is called tradition.

Two words that are often thought to have the same meaning are *bravery* and *courage*. However, these words have very different meanings.

Bravery is most times a single action that comes about because you have run out of any other options: charging up a hill, jumping on a grenade, climbing a high wall, putting yourself in the line of fire to save others, etc. These are brave actions, but they are singular and, for the most part, of a short duration.

Courage, on the other hand, is a sustained quality of character. You aren't courageous for a short time and then it is over. Courage is a virtue that comes from deep within your soul.

You may know what a brave man stands for because he will tell you. A man of courage will *show* you what he won't stand for. This is much more important.

A man of courage knows and loves the truth. He lives it every day. It is at the center of his existence. He has that rare gift: the ability to live what he says he believes every day. His actions are always consistent with his words.

The courageous person doesn't wait to see what others may do and then act. Courageous men and women defend leadership. They are the first to arrive and the last to leave.

With courageous people, others come first. They embody all of the other virtues, but honor is always front and center in their lives. They are either loved or hated; there is no middle ground. They are loved and respected by those whom they serve and protect. On the other hand, people of virtue are often hated by weak and feeble souls who lack the strength of character and conviction of their beliefs to be courageous, and who are made to appear weak when compared to those chosen few with real courage and honor.

Courage knows no age, sex, height, race, or ability. Anyone who faces each day willing to give all that they can, all of the time, qualifies to be called courageous.

Each and every one of us in our daily lives is called to this state, without ever realizing what we are doing. Each of you here listening to my words demonstrates that you wish to be courageous by wearing your virtues as a uniform. It calls you away from the ordinary, the everyday, and the crowd. It unites you with others like yourself, those seeking to maintain a tradition of excellence that has made America the greatest nation on this earth and the greatest nation known in history. By being here you say that you not only agree with this tradition but that you find it valuable enough to maintain and pass on to others. If you are living the virtues only for what they can do for you, then you should leave and be silent. Rather, you should be wearing it because it represents in a concrete way what you are and the things you believe and hold sacred.

If you aren't something without your wealth, skills, gifts, and talents, you will never be anything with them. It is never a matter of what you put on, it is a matter of what you put in it that counts most. The uniform won't make you brave, honorable, or courageous, but it will affirm to others that you have these qualities and virtues. You should never do anything that would bring your uniform into question or tolerate others that do. You are not in a club or on a team; you belong to a brotherhood, a family. You must share each other's joys and sorrows, compensate for each other's weaknesses, and share your strengths. You must see a common goal that has very little to do with individual honors or titles.

The number of medals on your chest doesn't make you a great man or woman. Only the medals in your heart, given by your fellow travelers, will have that power, those virtues. When you leave here, some of you will have been honored in an individual way. But remember: no one got here alone. Each one here shares in the glory of the other. Celebrate your accomplishment, but also celebrate one another. Be joyful that you have what most of the people in the world seek and want: fellowship. Know that if you ever need something there will always be a fellow traveler there with a hand extended to help. You are never alone.

To paraphrase a quote from William Shakespeare's "King Henry V":

And whenever this day shall pass, we in it shall be remembered. We few, we happy few; we band of brothers. For he who sheds his blood with me shall be my brother. And men in country now abed shall think themselves accursed that they were not here, and hold their manhoods cheap while any speaks, who fought with us upon this day!

One of my great joys here today, is that in a time when this world needs honor most, I see and know so many honorable people!

LET US REMEMBER - FOR WE HAVE SO MUCH TO REMEMBER

(Given at the dedication of the Alleghany County (Pa.) Veterans Memorial and Library, April 2010)

In the autumn of 1863, President Abraham Lincoln found himself in a small town in central Pennsylvania. He had come to be part of a group of people dedicating a new national cemetery for those men who had fought and died at the Battle of Gettysburg. Since Lincoln is one of my great American Heroes, I will be using some of his quotes from that day.

As it turns out, Lincoln and I have many things in common. For instance, we are almost the same height: he was 6' 4 ½" inches tall and I am 5' 7". For a former Marine officer, that is really not that far apart.

Lincoln wasn't the featured speaker that November day. He had been invited almost as an afterthought. He was asked to make a few appropriate remarks. His speech followed that of the greatest public speaker of his day; a man by the name of William Everett. Everett had spoken for two and a half hours about the great Greek heroes and their many battles and glorious deaths.

Lincoln then stood and spoke for two and a half minutes. And in that short time what he said changed this great nation forever. His words still echo and resonate purely in our history today as much as they did the moment he first spoke them.

Earlier in his career Lincoln had talked about the power of words. He said that words were the only device that was available to mankind that could communicate to those who had already died, those who were now living, and to those human beings yet to be born. This is exactly what you are doing here on this very spot here at this very moment. You are very eloquently speaking to the past, present, and the future.

There is a great deal of difference between the meaning of the terms *to recall* and *in remembrance*. *To recall* means to think about the past and what occurred. *In remembrance* means something much more sacred; it means *to make present again*. To make present again! It means to actually stand in the past with those you are celebrating. Without realizing the true majesty of your actions, you here are a living definition of an idea put forth by the German philosopher Hegel. He coined the idea of a zeitgeist, a time spirit, a time guardian. This is what this grove, this monument is really all about. You now stand with them. Their deeds are *your* deeds. Their honor is *your* honor.

When I was a history teacher, I would ask my new classes every September to name for me the greatest tool available to mankind for building civilizations. Then I would ask these same students to name the greatest weapon that human beings have at their disposal to destroy civilizations? They would suggest many diverse and different kinds of things, but were always stunned when I gave them my answer to those two very basic questions. I truly believe that the greatest tool and the greatest weapon are exactly the same thing: words.

Every human institution, whether it be a government, religion, social, or cultural group is built on a foundation of only the power and meaning of words. America is not simply a place on this earth, a land mass with water and trees. America is much more than this. America is a grand idea; a great and ongoing experiment born in the hearts and minds of our Founding Fathers. This gathering of so many great men who were in love with the idea of a virtuous nation, a virtuous people, was never seen before and has never been known since this time.

Virtues are a very special kind of word that defines a very different kind and context of existence. Because we live in a material world, we are condemned to definitions. Every object in this world is named, described, and defined in such a way that even when the object is not present to us every person can still call an image to mind (e.g., house, car, cat, etc.) But this is a vocabulary or a language, if you like, that will only support concepts in this and of this material world. There is an entirely different class of words not of this material world but of a higher and greater existence. These words, these ideas are called virtues. They are known to each and every person but they call to mind no single material concept as ordinary words do. Each of us defines these virtues in the most personal place of our being in our heart, our spirit and our soul. Honor, duty, loyalty, freedom, liberty and love are but a few of the virtues upon which this great nation is built. This almost spiritual language that are virtues and that each person must learn to speak in their actions can only be learned from observation the virtuous actions of others. If virtue is not seen in action, it is not taught; therefore, it is not learned.

All virtues grow from one basic simple human concept: respect. All we demand of ourselves as a nations and require of the world as a whole is simple respect! We as Americans ask nothing more, and as history has taught us, we will accept nothing less.

The greatest of these virtues is honor! Without honor a person can never be virtuous, for personal honor is the very foundation of each citizen of this nation and of the very nation itself. Our Founding Fathers had a passionate love for this concept of personal honor. It is our highest calling and duty, and the actions that result from this highest of virtues makes all things and people it reaches and touches sacred. *Honored dead* and *hallowed ground* are no longer simply hollow phrases.

One of my favorite writers in all of history is man who almost no one else has ever heard or read about or at least has never heard his name. This man lived in what is now the country of Holland almost 400 years ago, and his name was Desiderius Erasmus. What makes him so special was that he was the first man to ever publicly think, say, and write that, as individuals, every human being was worthy of dignity and respect; that all human beings had worth and value, not because the state granted them these rights and honored principles, but by the very fact that they were people and that their very existence granted and accorded them this dignity and respect. Therefore, every nation and state had not only the duty but the obligation to protect and secure the rights of its people. This security and protection was our greatest birthright as human beings.

Many men through the last 400 years, such as the great political philosophers Locke and Hobbs, have written about this concept with different interpretation of a person's worth and value and their relationship to and with the state to which the serve.

Yet it was an obscure Virginia farmer and philosopher who dared for the first time in human history to actually put these ideas on paper and to state a nation's obligation to secure and protect them as a matter of national honor and duty, and as a reason for that nation's very existence. This man's name was Thomas Jefferson, and what he wrote was this:

"We hold these truths to be self-evident, that all men are created equal, that they are endowed by their Creator with certain unalienable Rights, that among these are Life, Liberty and the pursuit of Happiness."

The egg that Erasmus laid, that was hatched by Jefferson, is called humanism, and that the United States of America is the first and only nation in the history of mankind to be founded upon these plain and simple yet most essential truths. Men have the right to liberty and freedom because they are men, not because the state grants it to them! Individuals are greater than laws, governments, and even nations. For all of these institutions were established on earth to serve human beings, not for individuals to serve governments or legal systems. We have not always understood this concept perfectly, but we are always working to perfect it in actuality.

This virtue of honor is not exclusive to America even though we were the first to found a nation using this principle. In England during the 1600s they also went through a Civil War that tore their country apart as all civil wars do. All of the people, both those born high and low, had to choose sides between their parliament and their king. One of those men who fought on the side of his king, even though he knew it was a lost cause, was a man named Richard Lovelace. His lover was a beautiful lady named Lucasta, and she couldn't understand why he said that he must side with the king and why he must fight where his heart led him! (Sound familiar?)

So Lovelace put his heartfelt reason in a very short poem and left it on her pillow the morning that he left to fight with his ruler. It was called "To Lucasta, On Going To The Wars" and it said:

Tell me not, Sweet, I am unkind,
That from the nunnery
Of thy chaste breasts, and quiet mind,
To war and arms I fly.

True, a new mistress now I chase,
The first foe in the field;
And with a stronger faith embrace
A sword, a horse, a shield.

Yet this inconstancy is such,
As you too shall adore;
I could not love thee, Dear, so much,
Loved I not honor more.

Honor more! This is the motto that should be written on the heart and soul of every citizen of our country. We have not only told the world but also demonstrated in every second of our sacred history as a nation that *we as a people and as a nation will have death before we will allow dishonor*!

As a young boy I can still remember when I heard a truly great man say these thrilling and passionate words:

122

"Let the word go forth from this time and place, to friend and foe alike, that the torch has been passed to a new generation of Americans..." – John Fitzgerald Kennedy

I have observed our nation over the years since I heard these words spoken, and I am proud to say that at times like this that torch is still burning brightly. You by your passion to honor all those who have freely chosen to serve our nation also made the conscious decision to pass that torch to *your* future and have done so magnificently.

If we search we will not find the greatness of our nation in our strongest citizens. To find our greatness you must seek the actions of our strongest and most capable citizens in their effort to protect the lives, value, worth, rights, and liberty of our weakest citizens. That is America's true greatness. Each of us must examine our lives and make a conscious choice not simply to contribute to the greatness of our country but to make a free and passionate choice to be committed to the *maintenance* and *security* of this greatness. We again swear an oath on that sacred honor we hold most dear, to never let anyone at any time, foe or friend alike, try in any way or form to harm or devalue even one or our citizens.

We made a sacred public pledge registered in the history of every nation of this world, that any person or group of persons with a love of our virtues of honor, liberty, and freedom could count on our help and dedication at any time and in any place to help them secure these blessings for themselves and their families, now and for their future. The only way that we can stand alone in this hostile world is to stand together. We must again pledge our word and bond to each other every day that we are ready to make the ultimate sacrifice not for land, not for riches, not for power, but simply to protect each other and to always secure and to pass to the next generation these virtues, upon which our nation was founded.

We are still the only nation on this earth where people will risk their lives and fortunes to belong and to live freely. This is truly the "American Dream." It is not a dream to become rich, powerful, or great. The American Dream is to be able to dream and to have a guarantee of a free opportunity to make these dreams come true for you and your children.

All dreams are made of three parts: The mystical, the magical, and the material. Here in this country we still have these resources in abundance. Our freedom and liberty serves as a beacon to the world that seems to be growing ever darker that here at least is still one place where dreams will be protected and where they can still come true.

Each of us must ask ourselves only four questions to uphold this honor this place of dreams this personal quest of virtue:

1. What is worth living for?
2. What is worth giving my life for?
3. What and where is the truth of what I believe found?
4. What are the bounds of my duty to protect my personal honor and that of my country?

It may sound strange, but one of the things that I learned in the Marine Corps was what it took to die like a hero. I found that it took but a moment of great personal bravery. Then I could be called a hero. In some situations I wouldn't even have time to make that choice—it would just happen. Living like a hero means that you have strength of character, not simply to keep telling people what you stand for. You also have the moral courage to show people what you won't stand for. This is another example of virtue in action.

What I learned that was much more important in my life was how to *live* like a hero. I found out how much courage and commitment it takes to make every action you perform consistent with every word you speak. This takes total commitment, every second of every minute of every day of your life.

Contribution is but a one-time yes, and then it is over. Commitment takes an ever-constant yes for every moment for the rest of your life.

If you want to know the difference between contribution and commitment, look no further than breakfast: ham and eggs! The chicken made the contribution; the pig mad the *commitment*.

Each and every person who has worked on this project here in this honored and sacred place has demonstrated that they know this difference very well, as it will also be known by all who come after you.

You have stated here at this place and time that any person who freely chooses to serve their country, that any person who chooses freely to defend their country, and that if any person that honor so demands that they are to die for their country, all will know that none of the actions and choices were ever done in vain. You have made, by this place, a public vow and pledge that they will never be forgotten.

Again, to paraphrase Lincoln on that November day in 1863: That from these honored people we will dedicate and commit ourselves to that great and honorable cause for which they were so devoted.

One of the great weapons for the preservation of our nation and all that it stands for and won't stand for can be found in the passion of its citizens. There must be no area of our great nation and its entire people about which we are not passionate. Just as it is with the relationship between two individuals who profess to love each other, where there is a passion and anxiety for the future welfare of both, so it is and must be with the relationship between of every citizen and their country! As you can see, there is nothing in my life for which I have more passion than for my country, except my family. I love my country and all of its people with my whole heart, my whole soul and spirit, and with every breath I take!

Some people from other parts of the world and other belief systems who observe my actions and listen to my words may call me a fanatic. I thank them and then, as simply and as calmly as possible, I respond to their criticism by explaining to them that they are just unfamiliar with the actions and voice of a true patriot.

It is such a great joy and comfort to know at this time in our history, when this country and the rest of the world must have and see real and true examples of great and honorable actions, that I can look out among all of you gathered here and see so many honorable people. We now should offer a constant prayer that God will always bless these men and women to whom this memorial is dedicated and that He will bless and comfort their families. That God will bless all of us and all those who come after us who freely choose honor as their journey and mission in life.

But most importantly we pray that God will continue to bless and honor the United States of America!

VETERANS DAY SPEECH

(Given Nov. 11, 2013, at the University of Pittsburgh, Johnstown Campus)

My Fellow Citizens...

We are gathered here this day, at this time and place, not to celebrate but to *commemorate*; not to rejoice but to *remember*. We are here to pay tribute not just to the veterans of the past, but to those of today and the heroes of the future.

We are here to honor the virtue of honor itself, for honor is the singular virtue that defines who and what heroes truly are. This is the virtue that defines veterans and sets them apart from the common and ordinary. It is the power that makes all veterans heroes.

"These are the times that try men's souls. The summer soldier and the sunshine patriot will, in the crisis, shrink from the service of his country."

This quote was written many years ago by a great man at a time when we were not yet a nation. It was written by Thomas Payne in his work called the "American Crisis".

Our country has often been in crisis. How we confront a crisis is one of the of the many factors that defines who and what we are as a nation and as a people.

A nation, a country, is not simply a place marked on a map; a political distinction or boundary. A nation, a country, is a noble idea born in the minds of great men who have the courage of heart and the virtue of character to dream that which no one else dares to dream possible; to do that which seems undoable; to reach for that which is unreachable.

Their determination of will and character of virtue brought our nation into existence. This is something that small men with a little imaginations and faint hearts can *never* comprehend or achieve.

The United States of America was born in the minds and hearts of these great visionaries. These giants brought that nation into being by sheer force of will. They took that dream and, by the application of character, made the dream into a vision of how the world could and should be. For there is no greater power found in the history of mankind than when people with dreams meet leaders with vision. For then the impossible becomes the possible; the unattainable is reached; the overwhelming is overcome.

These giants understood that heralded phase. They understood in their minds, hearts and souls that they were standing on the very threshold of history, daring to hope beyond hope. They dared to believe that a nation of ordinary people could live their lives as freely as God had created them to live and to be; that it was within their power and character to create a new world where with courage, determination, and virtue a free people could govern themselves. Their love of liberty and freedom was only equaled by their hatred of tyranny, despotism, and injustice. As they themselves proclaimed, they pledged their very fortunes, their lives, and their sacred honor to this task of a new nation in a new world.

We are the children and heirs of those great men. We are citizens of that great nation, that noble experiment, that awesome dream, that sacred vision. Freedom is our birthright and liberty is our inheritance.

In our history, we as a nation, as a people, haven't always done what is right and good the first time we have tried. Like all children, our nation has not always made the best choices at first. But in the history of a nation, as in every individual life, wisdom most often comes from poor judgment and from introspection after failure from a crisis overcome.

We have always tried with all our heart and will to rectify our shortcomings. We have tried with all of our heart and will to fulfill that great destiny purchased and willed to us by those giants who dared to dream our nation and its citizens into being. This dream was born and tried in the crucible of conflict and crisis. This dream, this vision, has had to be protected always by men of equal honor and character. For *any* dream of liberty, *any* vision of freedom, is a natural enemy to evil. The natural enemy of those persons and people determined to subjugate and enslave the mind and spirit the very *life* and *soul* of ours and any great nation founded on virtue.

These heroes willing to protect this dream every day and at any cost demanded since the very beginning of our nation have been called patriots. They are our veterans. These exceptional people also take an oath of honor to preserve and protect that dream and sacred vision with their very lives if necessary. They have freely pledged their future to this nation as it is and as it can be.

Our nation is *not* our government. It is our people. It is a living nation. A changing nation. A growing nation. But what must *never* change are the principles upon which this nation is founded. These basic freedoms and rights must never be allowed to be perverted or prostituted by any individual or individuals who lust for power or who possess an insidious desire of greed!

Veterans are and have always been the very watchdogs of these rights and freedoms. They have always been willing to go anywhere at any time and to do everything that is possible to protect and preserve this nation that they and we love and cherish so much!

There are many so-called leaders today that are willing to tell you what they stand for. But in doing this they tell and show us *nothing* about their character and virtue as men.

Veterans, on the other hand, have the understanding and love of honor and the iron will of virtue to *show* the world and history what they will not stand for. This singular attribute and quality tells and shows us everything we will ever need to know about their virtue and character.

We do not gather here this day to grieve for what we have lost as a nation by the sacrifices of these hero veterans. We are here to collectively remember and give value and worth to what we have gained as a nation by the actions, dedication, and honorable deeds of these hero veterans.

Honor is a mute virtue; it is only given a voice in history by the honorable actions of honorable people. Veterans are these honorable people! Their lives are not silent lives; their deeds are not silent deeds. Because even if we don't know their individual names, the great history of our nation has recorded their collective actions of honor in the very fiber and fabric of our being of our great country and of the collective identity of our national character.

Many of these heroes have been called upon to give their very lives for this nation. This dream, this vision, and this sacrifice is said to be tragic. And it is. But this ultimate sacrifice only becomes a *tragedy* if we the living allow their sacrifice of honor to be forgotten. If we are not inspired and motivated to follow them. This is why it is imperative that we gather together here today at this time and place to keep their memory alive. By doing so, we forever keep these heroes in our hearts. For this is what gives our great nation its soul.

In history the greatest good has always demanded the best of men, and by their sacrifices of honor these veterans are lifted to the heights of that very greatness.

To paraphrase another great American hero... We must here and now in this place, at this moment, resolve that these heroes shall not have served, sacrificed, lived, and died in vain. Because we here and now in this place and in every corner of this great nation must rededicate ourselves every day to that dream and vision that has been entrusted to them and to each of us; that that dream and vision that they have protected throughout the life of our nation with the greatest of honorable actions possible.

We here this day and at this place must also pledge our sacred honor, our lives, our future resolve to each other that this great nation will forever have a constant rebirth of freedom and liberty under God; that our nation, which is and will always be governed by the people, for the people, and with people shall never perish from this earth!

We must resolve and pledge that the great light of liberty and freedom will never dim or fade but forever shine as a beacon for the entire world and will ever illuminate the constant and dangerous loving path of liberty and human freedom of mind, body, will, spirit, and soul!

We must live our lives as models and examples of virtue and honor. Our actions must always every day be consistent with what we say we believe, so that this truth that we hold so dear will inspire every generation that is to come after us to raise up among their populations such heroes ever willing to freely give all to protect all.

If we do this with all of our heart and soul, with our spirit and sacred honor, then we give the greatest honor to these veterans, these heroes, these giants. So that vision, that dream, that they and we hold so dear will never die.

I ask God to bless you. I ask God bless all veterans everywhere and for all time. I ask God to forever bless America with such heroes. And I ask God to protect, preserve, and inspire us and our great nation forever to be an honorable and faithful people, and that we will always be truly worthy of all that we have been given, and to protect and defend all that has been entrusted to our care!

WHO WILL SING MY SONG

Sing for me not a sad song.
But for me a song with a melody so sweet
That each and every note
Has been graced and kissed by the sun.
Let each measure and line
Speak of my wishes and dreams.
Let each chord tell of my faith and hope.
Sing verses of my smiles and laughter
Of my tears and joys.
Save the sweetest words to tell
Of my friends and my loves
My noise and my silence.
Let the harmonies celebrate
 My plans and journeys my highs and lows.
Let it end with the story of
The height of my spirit
The depth of my soul.
Finish my song with this refrain:
That I had finally found true freedom
That I had finally learned to fly.
When you sing my song together or alone
You will find truth and comfort
In these words:
I am always very near
I never really died.

NATURE AND PRAYER

In quiet humble silence
Nature teaches all who will but watch her
To pray in a way that is most pleasing to God.
Soft, warm spring winds
Gently play the creator's quiet music.
The new blades of green grass and the leaves on great and little trees
Gracefully dance and their movement
Pays humble homage to the Master of all creation.

The flowers and blossoms scream
With their colors of thanks
While crickets and frogs
Raises a symphony of song
To their heavenly Father.

Mountains and valleys
Offering up their height and many shades of green and white
While swiftly running streams and mighty rivers and oceans
Offer up their cold and wet
Their never ending tide and currents.

Natural prayer is not of words or of deeds.
The prayer of nature is always that of simplicity!
It is the prayer of just being.

"IF" (FOR TODAY)
(My apologies to Mr. Kipling)

If you have never taken the time to watch the sunrise or sunset, you never know true beauty; for these are the standard by which all beauty must be measured.

If you have never looked to the heavens on a bright starry night and found yourself speechless, you have never known the beauty and delicacy that is found in the balance and order of nature.

If you can watch injustice and not feel the whips and chains that beat and bind another unfairly, you do not know the true depth of nor deserve true freedom or liberty.

If you can watch others serve in your place and mock their service, then you do not know the depth and definition that is HONOR.

If you can see children unfed and unclothed and not feel their pains or their cold, nor try to remedy their condition, you do not know the responsibility that comes with being a member of mankind.

If you are blinded by your ambitions and greed to the point that they become the center of your existence, then you have lost the moral compass of your life.

If the acquisition of power and fame are your life's purpose, you have really stopped living a valued, worthwhile, and meaningful life.

If your measure as a person is the adulation and compliments of others, you have sold yourself cheaply to the common market of humanity.

If you have never had or known the courage to stand, speak, and take ownership of your personal thoughts to those in power, you are still a child.

If you see the helpless and are not moved to change their plight, you are blind and deaf.

If you can stand by and watch while others are insulted, demeaned, and crushed by the powerful, then you are also the aggressor.

If you can't choose that which is right and just from that which is evil, you have never really found your soul.

If you are not the master of your own conscience and actions, then you are always to live as a slave.

If you have found nothing in your life that is worth defending with your life, you have never really lived.

If your life's goal has been to blend in rather than to stand out, you aren't an individual person.

If you have never found a cause that you are passionate about, you have no sense of art or creativity.

If you have never loved and cared for an animal, you don't know what unconditional love really is.

If you have never loved a friend as deeply a member of your God-given natural family, you have never known true friendship.

If you can't serve when and where you are most needed without the expectation of reward, you have no true sense of charity.

If you do not understand the need to protect the life, liberty, and freedom of others at all cost, then you can make no valid claim to life, liberty, or freedom for yourself.

If you can't tolerate other people worshiping as they please or choosing not to worship, you have no real faith.

If you never test or know your limits, you will never really know yourself.

If you have never found anything worth living or dying for in your life, you have never known true love.

If you can't say and mean these words from the depth of your being – "I forgive you" – then You will never know or feel true forgiveness.

If you can stand and watch another person's dreams shattered and trampled by the uncaring, and you don't help them sow new seeds of hope, you have no vision or faith in the future.

If, when you rise every morning, you have not examined your life so that you know what has truth, value, worth, and virtue within your own heart and soul, then you can't fill even one minute of that entire day with any worthwhile distance run!

TO FISH

The water swiftly runs its course
The white yellow sunshine
Dances lightly over each ripple.
The trees gently yield to the surface
Of the calm water,
For it is softly caressing the face of an old friend.
While under the depthless glaze
Slowly swims one of God's perfect creations.
With measured movements of his endless ballet
He gracefully glides through his domain.
Patiently he awaits the challenge from above.
This test of his lifetime
And his very life.
Putting to use all of the lessons
taught to him by his sole teacher; Nature.
Pitting him against those of his learned foe.
This Man with his rod.
Some people see fishing as simply a sport
when it is in reality a philosophy of life
a fulfillment of many natures
Man in his simplest element.

Being the one thing that God intended him to be
Joyful and Happy.
But the observer is left with a new
Eternal question!
Is it the man who lures the fish?
Or is it the fish that now
Lures the man?

THE OLD MAN LOOKING OUT TO THE SEA

There he stands facing the sea that constantly calls,
With his back to the land, cane in his hand.
This old one is reliving in silence
A life that went where ever
And whenever the sea called.
He is celebrating a spirit
That has seen so much beauty
That life offers to all who will but listen or see.
Yet few have the faith or courage
To answer this call.

All who don't know the wealth and hope
That is brought by true freedom,
They call him a foolish old man.
They scorn him because it appears to them
 He was never settled or tied to a place.
What they don't understand is that the
 Secret of his life was movement.
For him to kiss the stars,
He had to soar to the heavens.
He choose to love and serve the sea,

He felt the tender caress of each wave.
His heart felt the pull of the tides,
In faith and freedom's name he just let himself go.

He had tasted and known human love and kindness.
These passions filled his heart and spirit for a short time,
But his spirit and soul demanded greater food.
He needed to be at the pure islands
When baptized by the morning sun.
His heart and eyes yearned to see the snow-covered
mountains.
He had to know the calm of the sea with its violent storms.
The wind in the sails was the breath of his spirit.
His ears learned to hear and to recognize the song of the very
sea itself
And he could join in each verse and refrain.

This old man who always faces the sea,
His back to the land with his hat in his hand,
Is pitied by those who do not know or understand his graces.
To their observations and judgment
He has nothing to show
For his life lived.

It will only be when their time comes,
When it is their time to take their only and last voyage
That they can ever understand the value of his life.
They must leave behind all of that which they have known and
held.
All of that baggage which they called their material wealth.
They face this unknown ocean for the first time and see only
its void,
Its darkness and its bottomless depth.

They now face a terror they have never known before.
They cling to the land because they are terrified to leave.

Whereas the old man
Still carries within his heart and mind
All of the things his life purchased.
Those thousand tiny memories and details,
Of the simplicity, beauty, and majesty of all he has seen and
known.
He has faced both heaven and hell
So he knows no fear.
This old man with his hat in his hand,
Standing with his back to the land,
With his face to the sea,
He is not afraid of what lays beyond the land
In the vast sea.
Unlike the others he is not facing the unknown,
The old man is simply facing home.

THREE SWANS

Once when overburdened with
Worldly cares,
I sought to escape by a fog shrouded river.
There I could be truly alone in Spirit and Soul.
When suddenly
Through the mist appeared
Three stately swans.
They moved silently, majestically, effortlessly
Over the glass-like water
No ripple, no motion,
In an instant they
Were gone.
I was left standing on that bank
 Surrounded by the warm white mist,
Trying to understand the mystery
Of that moment.
Was it a ghost or a gift?
Dream or vision?
I then became aware my burden was gone
I was free
I was once more
Alone with myself and my God.

MY FRIEND

My Heart hears the caring Voice
Of your Presence in my life.
The sounds that ears can't always hear
Or Words that voices can't always speak.
That silent call which says I am in Need
And that action of your heart
That answers I Know and I am here.

The Perception that reaches past
Artificial walls and gates
Over heaps of clutter placed by
A Lifetime of hurts and disappointments.
The touch from your honest soul on my Spirit
That makes of life not a slum but a church
Not a Curse but a Sweet melody.
That which helps me to become
The best that I can be
Yet leaves me who I really am.

You Love without question or reward
You Reach without Fear of pain

You Share without counting the cost.
You always raise up and never tear down.
In My Life you are the living definition
Of all that is Found and All that is Held Best in
The simple words: You are my Friend!

THE GIFT OF ART

Man can create nothing.
God has reserved this singular power to Himself,
But to compensate
He graced some of His beings with the gift of art.
Art is the ability of these precious few people
To describe the acts of God's creation
In such a way
That the rest of mankind believes that.

GOD'S LOVE

There are no hidden treasures in God's love
Only secluded places where we would not think to look
These great treasures are found before us in plain sight
If left to ourselves we would have God dwell more in our mind
So it would be easy to understand and know by our intellect.
Instead He dwells in the hearts of all men
This gives each of us the same equality and the same demands
on His mercy and Love
We can then become equal in loving Him
He can therefore easily love each of us in return.
Not everyone can understand about the nature of God
What theologians call the science of God.
But everyone who has ever loved can know the love of God.
It is a much better thing to love God than to know God as
St. Thomas Aquinas tells us.
If it were left to our own devices, we wouldn't talk
Or associate with people we believe to be unlike ourselves
But again the wisdom of God is the folly of man.
God gives us a great the great choice of being made blind by
His light
A blind person can make no preconceived judgments about
any person they meet

But this is being blinded by the Love of God
We may still stumble and fall as in the blindness of darkness
Except With the blindness of light we can never lose our
direction or our goal.
Because God is that light that warmth that sweet fragrance we
always seek
The Spirit with His Grace always sees we rise and continue in
the right direction.
If left to us Christ would have been born in a palace
With an army encamped nearby
Ready to do his bidding and right all wrongs
Instead He came as a child
Lived a life of justice and peace
Preached compassion and forgiveness
He died a victim of love
He was one of us.
His Death released that light.
Some light separates day from night
We call this the sun.
From the cross the light that Christ gave destroys the darkness
forever,
We call this light the SON.
There are no hidden treasures in God's love
Only secluded places where we do not think to look.
We are those treasures that others seek
Those are the treasures that we find the hardest to discover.
Search blindly in the light and they are right in front of you
always.

ABOUT THE AUTHOR

Richard M. O'Bryan is a former history teacher and a retired member of the United States Marine Corps. When he's not working on his writing, he produces a YouTube vlog called "The Standup Philosopher" and is a regular contributor for YouNow.com. His book, *Josh and Me: "How Hard Can It Be?" The Mishaps and Misadventures of Two Best Friends*, is a collection of humorous tales base on O'Bryan's real-life experiences growing up. He is also a motivational speaker.

For more information, visit richardobryan.us.

A SELECTION FROM: JOSH & ME, "HOW HARD CAN IT BE?"

As soon as we were clear of the top, we found the missing kids sliding down that wet grass toward the bottom of that hill like they were on a toboggan at the Olympic Games. By the time we made contact with the grass, we were already speeding up and gaining on them. By the second bounce, the rope had tied Josh and me together in knots that would've made sailors proud. We began to tumble and roll, and each time we did, in would come one of those kids to us like fish on a line. Another roll and they were stuck to us like glue, with each one in some strange position. The first one was tied to my leg upside down, the second was attached to Josh's back sideways. Soon we were all together and gaining speed at the bottom of the slope.

There was only about ten feet between the bottom of the hill and the edge of the duck pond. We passed that point at light speed, hit the water, and skipped like a flat stone on a calm lake. It was four skips before we came to rest right in the middle of all the ducks. The water was about a foot deep, and beneath it were about ten inches of mud and fifty years of rotten food and duck droppings. Covered in this muck, we looked like a never-before-seen creature, with twenty-four arms, twenty-four legs and twelve heads.

Josh and Me: "How Hard Can It Be?" The Mishaps and Misadventures of Two Best Friends is available at your favorite bookstore.